TOTAL SURRENDER
TO THE WILL OF GOD

Samia Mary Zumout

All biblical extracts contained herein have been taken from *the New Revised Standard Version Bible: Catholic Edition, copyright © 1989, 1993.*

Book Cover Design: Ana Keyworth, Graphic Designer

Cross picture: ©Ana Keyworth taken in Medjugorje, Bosnia-Herzegovina

Dedicated To:

JESUS CHRIST
My Beloved Lord and Savior, My Healer, My Teacher,
My Strength, My Best Friend, My Confidant,
and My Role Model

Thank You very much for demonstrating through my life that
I can do ALL things through You.
I am nothing without Your Grace!
My life is fully Yours.

and

My Faithful Parents Elias and Sonia Zumout

Thank you very much for your selfless unconditional love,
for your support and sacrifices
throughout my life and especially during my illness!
I love you both more than words can express.

Acknowledgments

This book is the fruit of the love, support, and prayers of various people, to whom I am most grateful and love very much.

My beloved heavenly family: God (Father, Son and Holy Spirit), Blessed Mother Mary, my guardian, angel and all the saints.

My beloved earthly family: My parents Elias and Sonia, my siblings and their beautiful families, Sophie, Nabil, Sue, Ramzi, Ghada, Hana, Lili, Christina, Amy, Andrew and Giana; my aunts Samira Khoury, Fifi Hishmeh, Eva Hishmeh-Bishara, Nadia Saroufim and Laurice Hamarneh. Thank you very much for your unconditional love, support and prayers. I love you all very much.

Msgr. James Murphy, Former Vicar General of the Diocese of Sacramento (2008–2014): Thank you very much for your support, prayers, spiritual direction, and for writing the Foreword.

Ana Keyworth: Thank you for using the talents God gifted you with to design the covers of both of my books out of the generosity of your heart.

Maureen Kubasak: Thank you for taking the time to edit the entire manuscript. Thanks also to Nabil Zumout, Maureen Masters, Maria Leon and Marizol Ploché for your edits on various chapters.

Maria Elena Gutierrez and Raquel Arenz: Thank you Maria Elena for volunteering to translate my book into Spanish despite your busy life. Thank you Raquel for translating my first book along with Enrique Romero and for taking the time to edit the second one. May God reward you all abundantly for your sacrifices and love.

v

All my dear friends for your love, support and prayers especially: Fr. Thomas Keller, Lourdes Pereira, Wendy Mertens, Marizol and Vernel Ploché, and Raul Ramirez.

Radio Santísimo Sacramento staff, volunteers and listeners, especially: Eliana Plimpton, Lorena and Guillermo Albarran, Francisco and Isabel Del Castillo, Juan Carlos Paredes, and many others: Thank you for your prayers, friendship, support and assistance during my radio programs.

Deacon Jerry and Barbara Pauly: Thank you for all your prayers, love, and generous support of my ministry.

Teo and Juanita Gonzalez and the Farfan family: Thank you for your prayers, support and love throughout the years and especially during my missions to Mexico.

Estela and James Smith, Jose and Teresa Navarro, Raul Ramirez: Thank you for taking me to Mass and for your assistance.

Thanks to all the people who prayed or still pray for me.

Thanks to all the generous people who donated to my ministry.

Thanks to all the people who assisted me during my illness.

Table of Contents

Foreword

Samia Zumout must be one of the first people on the planet to write a book with one thumb, on a cell phone.

She did it that way because she had no choice. Her body has been so debilitated by multiple sclerosis (a disease that showed up quite unexpectedly when she was in her early forties) that she cannot perform the most simple tasks anymore. And with each passing day her condition gets worse.

At the time of writing this Foreword, she could not walk or drive. She could not wash or dress herself. Even something as simple as buttoning her shirt was too much because her fingers would not obey her brain anymore. So writing a book the normal way was out of the question.

But she did have one thumb that still functioned enough to form words on a cell phone, and she was determined to make use of it before even that remaining part of one hand ceased to function. The end result has been very worthwhile.

This is a book about the purpose of suffering. It is about how one soul was devastated by a doctor's diagnosis in 2011 but threw herself on her face before God and asked him for strength. It is about how she discovered that suffering has a purpose – our own spiritual growth and the salvation of others. It is about her discovery that prayer joined to sacrifice constitute the most powerful force in human history.

Incredibly, Samia is one of the most lighthearted people I know. She is totally at peace with God's will, despite her daily pain and complete loss of independence, and she actually treasures the lessons she had learned from her condition. She told me recently that if she were offered the choice of getting back her original health, while losing the lessons she has learned from that sickness, she would choose to keep the illness.

"Each day is a living miracle to me," she writes in Chapter 9, "and I have never felt such inner peace, joy and unconditional love for others. Today nothing separates me from the love of Christ."

Those are powerful words, coming from someone who suffers as much as she does. I can't think of a more important lesson for all of us—those of us who are sick and those of who are healthy. We all have some cross to bear in life but many of us miss the point. We don't see it as an opportunity to grow. And we don't think of it as something to be offered up for others. The result is a lot of suffering in this world goes to waste. That is the point of this book.

Monsignor James Murphy
Diocese of Sacramento
Feast of Christ the King 2014

Chapter 1

Suffering

"And not only that, but we also boast in our sufferings, knowing that suffering produces endurance, and endurance produces character, and character produces hope, and hope does not disappoint us, because God's love has been poured into our hearts through the Holy Spirit that has been given to us." — Romans 5:3—5

"If you knew that today was your last day on earth, what lessons from your life's experiences would you like to share with the world before you leave?"

These words echoed loudly within my soul in the middle of the night, shaking me out of my slumber. It was as if God was nudging me to make every effort to write this book that He had put on my heart a while back. God asks us but does not force us.

The truth is, I have been dreading writing the book due to my physical condition. In 2011, I was diagnosed with horrific medical diseases that have aggressively attacked my central nervous system, particularly my spinal cord: primary progressive multiple sclerosis (M.S.), cervical stenosis (neck), and myelopathy (spinal cord). Each disease alone is sufficient to leave any healthy person severely disabled in a very short span of time. Indeed, as I write this book in the fall of 2014, I have become fully disabled due to the extensive permanent damage to my central nervous system. I went from an extremely independent busy person, traveling constantly, to a very dependent person unable do the simplest tasks on my own. I can't

1

walk; I can't dress myself; I can't write or type except with my right thumb on my iPhone—which is how I am writing this book; I can barely feed myself and I certainly can't drive. I have become dependent on others to help me with all my basic needs. Every part of my body from my neck down to my feet is in severe debilitating pain, weakness, spasms, extreme fatigue, tremors, electric shocks and many other symptoms. The only words to describe my daily condition are: extreme physical suffering.

Ironically, emotionally and spiritually, I am the happiest and most peaceful I have ever been in my whole life.

Most people have a hard time understanding the last sentence. Even the people who see me can't understand how I can be joyful and peace-filled in the midst of so much suffering. Don't misunderstand me, I am not a masochist. I do not enjoy suffering. Nobody in their right mind does. Suffering however, is an inevitable part of our human experience while on earth. It is impossible to go through life without enduring one's share of suffering. We all suffer in different ways, whether it be physical, mental, emotional or spiritual.

All of us will face suffering, heartache and pain during our journey through life. What makes the difference in our journey is how we respond to the suffering. We can give up and become bitter and hateful, or we can hold onto our faith and deny ourselves. This requires that we die to our ego and the selfish pride that hinders us from discerning the will of God. We must pick up our cross with love and forgiveness like our Lord Jesus and continue on the very narrow path to heaven.

As a Christian who lives my faith and has fully surrendered my life to Christ, the following words of Jesus have become the foundation and spiritual guidance for my life: *"If anyone would come after me, let him deny himself and take up his cross daily and follow me. For whoever would save his life will lose it, but whoever loses his life for my sake will save it."* (Luke 9:23–24)

These powerful words are very challenging, especially since the world we live in is selfish and egocentric world. It's easier to avoid Jesus' cross and choose to focus only on His resurrection and ignore what it takes to be a follower of Christ.

Suffering was never part of God's plan for our lives. God is pure love and mercy. He does not rejoice in our suffering. It is the result of sin, whether it be original sin, our sin or the sin of others. Although we live in a fallen world that is still suffering from the consequences of sin, this world is governed by spiritual laws and not just physical ones. There is a spiritual aspect and consequence to everything we do in this physical world. In fact, the only way you will be able to understand my book is if you read it with your spiritual eyes.

Many people caught up in the material world go through life unaware of their spiritual being due to ignorance or forgetfulness. Consequently, they remain disconnected from God. The only thing that is true to them is the material world. If they can touch it, see it, taste it or smell it, then it is real. Since the spiritual cannot be seen, then it must not exist.

We will never understand Jesus' profound words above or the value of our suffering in this world if we only look at them through physical eyes. No wonder suffering is avoided at all cost whether it is through self-medication, various addictions or even in extreme cases, suicide.

The purpose of my book is to share with you what I have learned so far from my life's journey, not only the lessons from my physical suffering but also the lessons from my missionary work. In 2006, the Lord Jesus called me to surrender to Him my attorney position and other aspects of my life. This ultimately led to my International Inner-Healing Ministry prior to the onset of my disease. For clarification, I have not recently found God to ease my physical pain. I have been fully dedicated to Him for many years.

Several people I have spoken with since my illness ask me the question: "*Why would God let you suffer? You have been faithfully serving Him for many years.*" You might be wondering the same. People usually pray to God in a moment of need. Although there is nothing wrong with that, those whose prayers are not answered the way they hoped, or those who are afflicted and feel punished, turn away angrily from God thinking "*a merciful God would not allow this to happen!*" The majority of people share the view that it's not "fair" that those who cheat and renounce God are rewarded with riches and a good life, while the faithful are often afflicted with suffering.

That is how things may appear to us when only viewed with the physical eyes. The spiritual reality is quite different. I pray that my story will inspire you to look at the sufferings and challenges of your own life through spiritual eyes, shedding light on what's important, giving purpose and value to things that otherwise seem meaningless in our physical world.

Chapter 2

Journey Towards Surrender

"Do not be conformed to this world, but be transformed by the renewing of your minds, so that you may discern what is the will of God—what is good and acceptable and perfect." — Romans 12:2

I spent the first 13 years of my life in the country of Jordan before immigrating to the United States. I never imagined that someday I would leave my chosen profession as a lawyer, to become a missionary evangelizing the love of Christ! That was the furthest thing from my mind. Even though I was born and raised as a Catholic Christian, I had many fears related to speaking publicly about my faith in a country dominated by Muslims. Christians were only about 5% of the population, and I often suffered discrimination for being a minority. I grew up with many insecurities, fears, shame and lies about myself. This shaped who I believed I was for the initial 20 years of my life, falsely believing I was worthless, insignificant and inferior. Like other people in the world, I learned to mask how I felt about myself, pretending to be happy on the outside while bleeding profusely on the inside.

The turning point in my life occurred seven years after my family had immigrated to the United States. In 1990, I was a student at the University of California at Davis and was studying abroad in France for my third year. Over the summer vacation, I went backpacking throughout Europe with a couple of my friends. During the trip we traveled to Medjugorje, a village in the country of Bosnia-Herzegovina (formerly known as Yugoslavia) where our Blessed

Mother Mary has been allegedly appearing daily since 1981. We went there purely out of curiosity and not seeking a spiritual experience. Even though we were planning on staying in this village for less than 24 hours, a series of miraculous events occurred that changed the course of our trip and also the rest of my life. We ended up extending our trip to a full week and then departed to Greece to continue our adventure in Europe. However, my experience in Medjugorje was so powerful and life-changing that I couldn't continue my travels as previously planned. I canceled my original itinerary and returned to Medjugorje for two more weeks, hungry for God.

I won't give a full account in this book about the sequence of miraculous events that transpired there, as I have previously chronicled those in my first book, *"The Bridge Between the East and West: A Journey to Truth through His Love."* These experiences included my childhood and upbringing in Jordan, my family's immigration to the United States in 1983 and my spiritual conversion in Medjugorje in 1990, which led to my spiritual awakening and inner-healing journey. I surrendered my life to God by leaving my secure job as a lawyer in 2006, and finally becoming a missionary living off of Divine Providence. The book narrated the lessons I learned about God's immense love for all of us and the emotional wounds we carry in our hearts that prevent us from allowing His love to heal us. If you are interested in finding out more about the events that led me to leave everything, to serve the Lord Jesus full-time, I strongly recommend you read it.

For a deeper understanding of this current book, I have highlighted two events in Medjugorje that greatly impacted my life. Before I do that, however, it is important to explain to my non-Catholic readers what Catholics believe concerning the Eucharist, what Eucharistic Adoration means, and how this relates to my story.

The Holy Eucharist is the sacrament that Jesus established when He took bread and wine, blessed them, and declared them to be His Body and Blood (Luke 22:17–20). He commanded His disciples: *"Do this in memory of Me."* He had earlier foretold that His presence in the

Eucharist would be real and substantial: *"I am the living bread that came down from heaven; whoever eats this bread will live forever ... Whoever eats My flesh and drinks My blood has eternal life, and I will raise him on the last day. For My flesh is true food, and My blood is true drink"* (John 6:51, 54–55). When a Catholic priest follows this command of Jesus and speaks the words of consecration at Mass, the bread and wine are permanently changed and they become Jesus: His Body, Blood, Soul, and Divinity. Eucharistic Adoration is the worship of Jesus Christ present in the Holy Eucharist. In churches that have this adoration, the Eucharist is displayed in a special holder called a monstrance, and people come to pray and worship Jesus continually throughout the day and often the night.

Returning to my story, the first event transpired one evening while praying inside St. James Church during Eucharistic Adoration. Even though I was born and raised Catholic, I had never previously participated in Eucharistic Adoration and I didn't know what to expect. But I had an open heart. I was kneeling in prayer when I started experiencing an incredible feeling of love that completely overwhelmed me. It was as if God's love engulfed me. I started sobbing and continued to cry for two hours. As I knelt down, I allowed my head to drop to the floor as I wept and wept, forming a small puddle of water all around me. My weeping was not caused by any sadness, but by an emotion that was foreign to me. I felt this intense heat within my heart and the rest of my body, feeling extremely loved like never before. God's love was cleansing and purifying me from the inside out. His immense love consumed my heart and began to heal many emotional wounds and insecurities. Suddenly, I heard a soothing voice within my soul resonating these healing words: *"The love that you are experiencing now is only a small token of the love that took Me to lay My life on the cross for you personally."* At that moment, I knew beyond a shadow of a doubt that Jesus was alive and was pure love. I also knew that He died for me personally, which meant that I was not worthless, inferior or unimportant as I had always falsely believed. His love and truth-filled words were bringing my spirit back to life.

7

Up until that moment, although born and raised Christian, I never had a personal relationship with Jesus. That night, I felt Jesus so deeply in my heart that I knew, for the first time in my life, the extent of His love for me. I knew that He died for me personally, just like He did for everyone else, including you, regardless of your religion or background. I experienced a glimpse of what would await us in heaven and I had tasted a piece of heaven while still on earth. This was the first time in my life that I was not afraid to die.

The second event also took place while I was in deep prayer in the Eucharistic Adoration Chapel. Again, I heard Jesus' voice deep within my heart asking me the following question: *"Would you give me your yes?"* I had no idea what His question entailed as Jesus didn't provide me with any further additional information. At first I thought He might be calling me to become a nun, as I innocently thought this was the only way I could serve God as a woman. I always had planned to become a lawyer to help people. At that moment, I responded wholeheartedly: *"Yes Lord Jesus! Whatever You ask me, I give You my yes. Just never allow me to walk away from You. Give me a clear sign of what You're asking of me."* At that moment, I offered my life and surrendered my will to God, ready to do His will. I sensed in my heart that my life was not going to be what I always imagined it to be, married by age 26, having 3 or 4 children and living a normal life dedicated to my family first, followed by my career.

It took 16 years of physical, emotional and spiritual preparation for me to realize what my "yes" involved. During these years, God showed me clearly that I needed to become a lawyer and not a nun. I worked extremely hard to put myself through law school, incurring huge student loans that practically suffocated me after graduation. I worked many long hours in a private corporation for over eight years. However, I was gaining much needed life experience.

Although these years were intense years of spiritual growth, Jesus was working on healing my soul from many emotional wounds, fears, lies, shame, brokenness and trust issues. Unbeknownst to me, I was being prepared and trained for my calling as an inner-healing prayer-minister, evangelizing His healing love to His wounded children. To accomplish that, Jesus had to start the healing process in me first, before I could help others. What gave me the necessary strength to go through this were all the spiritual tools and discipline that our Blessed Mother Mary had taught me in Medjugorje. I placed Jesus at the center of my life. My day always started with Mass. I had a disciplined prayer life, fasted frequently, confessed my sins regularly and, read the Bible and other spiritual books. Jesus became my best friend, my healer, my confidant, my teacher and my role model on how to live my life as His follower. I couldn't imagine my life without Him. I lived for Him and He gave meaning to everything in my life.

In April 2006, while I was deep in prayer in the Eucharistic Adoration Chapel in church, I heard Jesus telling me that the time had come to fulfill my "yes" to Him. He was asking me to surrender to Him everything I knew, my profession, my independence, my finances and even my heart's desires. Jesus said: "*The time has come. Do you trust in My love for you to surrender your whole life to Me? Do you trust that I would provide you with all your daily needs?*" I was very grateful at that point that He had already healed me of my trust issues. I responded affirmatively, asking Him to give me the graces necessary to fulfill His will in my life.

I was certain of God's love for me. He is my Heavenly Father who is pure love, and He would never ask anything of me that was not for my benefit. I knew that if I lived according to God's will, everything in my life, no matter how painful or difficult, would serve its perfect purpose for my own spiritual growth and for the fulfillment of my mission on earth.

I took the biggest leap of faith in my life into the unknown. I resigned from my secure career not knowing what was in store for me. Thankfully, I had moved back to my parents' home several months earlier so I didn't have to worry about paying for rent, utilities or my food. I was 36 years old at the time, and in the eyes of the world and the people who knew me, it looked like I had completely lost my mind. The world defined success in terms of material prosperity, prestigious careers, financial independence and power. These were precisely the things that Jesus was asking me to surrender to Him. He was showing me that worldly success was temporary, often empty and self-serving. True success that lasted for all eternity was not measured by material wealth, titles or power but by how much we obediently submitted ourselves to God's will in our lives!

Of course, it was a very humbling and painful process to teach me detachment from all my worldly securities. I was learning firsthand what it meant to "deny myself" to follow Christ in my life. I had to die to my own plans, ego, financial independence and people's opinion of me. Ironically, I felt a sense of freedom and inner peace that surpassed human understanding. I was being set free!

Chapter 3

The Unfolding of the Mission

"For surely I know the plans I have for you, says the Lord, plans for your welfare and not for harm, to give you a future with hope."
—Jer. 29:11

Leaving my career as a lawyer didn't mean I had wasted my legal education by following God's will for my life. It was quite the contrary. There was a purpose for it, as it gave me credibility when I later spoke publicly or evangelized during my missionary work. The Lord Jesus was using it for His purpose and in His own way. I was "practicing law" in a spiritual manner as I was fighting for souls! I couldn't imagine doing anything more important than that. Each human life is priceless to Jesus. It cost Him every drop of His Precious Blood. All the hardships I had undergone served their purpose for my spiritual growth and pulled me as close to Jesus as possible.

After I resigned from my job, I attended Mass every day and then spent a minimum of three to four hours in deep prayer in the Eucharistic Adoration Chapel. I needed to remain united to Jesus through prayer to discern His will and remain strong spiritually. The first task that Jesus asked me in prayer was to write my first book *The Bridge Between the East and West: A Journey to Truth through His Love*. Jesus confirmed to me that writing this book was an important part of my life's mission as it would bring people closer to His heart; many would experience His healing love while reading about my inner-healing and faith journeys. Through my openness about my brokenness and the journey that led me to Him, Jesus would speak to open hearts, filling them with His liberating truth and healing love. He added that it would only take me 30 days to write the book if I lived a sacramental life centered on the Eucharist, spent three hours daily in Eucharistic Adoration, prayed the 20 mysteries of the Rosary daily and fasted on bread and water throughout that period. Indeed, when I was ready to start writing, I began on July 17, 2007 and the book was completed on August 15, 2007—exactly 30 days later.

When I finished writing, I wept tears of relief and joy, as writing this book was healing for me! Looking back at my life made me realize that each detail had been so meticulously designed by God. There had been no coincidences. Even all the hardships or suffering I had endured throughout my life were crucial steps in pulling me closer to Christ, making me stronger by molding me into the person I was. Every aspect of my life reflected His great love for me. I realized that my mission on earth was to guide others back to our Heavenly Father's loving heart, by being one of the many instruments and messengers of His healing love.

Within one month, I found a small Catholic publishing company that was very interested in publishing my book. This was miraculous, given that I was a new unknown author. My book spoke profoundly to the owner of the company. He agreed to publish it with the condition that I would obtain an Imprimatur from my local Catholic Diocese. (An imprimatur is an official declaration by the local bishop that a manuscript does not contain anything that contradicts the Catholic Church's teachings.) I immediately submitted the manuscript of my book to my diocese for review. Unfortunately, the process was so lengthy that it was taking over 18 months. By then, I had lost my publisher due to financial constraints. Apparently, God had a different publisher in mind and a later time for publishing. I just needed to be patient and await the unfolding of God's plan.

Chapter 4

A Special Commissioning

"My brothers and sisters, whenever you face trials of any kind, consider it nothing but joy, because you know that the testing of your faith produces endurance; and let endurance have its full effect, so that you may be mature and complete, lacking in nothing."
— James 1: 2–4

In June 2008, I received a call from a priest friend from another state who knew that I had left my career to serve God; I will call him "Father (Fr.) Ben." He invited me to come to his parish for one year to bring my Inner-Healing Prayer Ministry to his English-and Spanish-speaking parishioners. Spanish was one of the four languages that I spoke fluently—besides English, French and Arabic. The Lord Jesus confirmed to me in prayer that this was His next step for me. Fr. Ben offered me a free room in a former convent in the same town and a stipend to pay for my personal expenses. Just as Jesus promised, He was providing for my daily needs.

My year was extremely intense, probably one of the most difficult years of my life spiritually! It felt like a continuous and rigorous spiritual boot camp. A few days after my arrival, the Lord Jesus revealed to me His primary reason for my new mission. Perhaps if He had disclosed this to me prior to my going, I would not have gone. I might have hesitated, thinking I wasn't qualified for the mission as it would have been too painful and overwhelming to bear. Initially, I wasn't planning on writing about this particular situation due to its sensitivity and how much pain it caused myself and others, spiritually and emotionally. I also didn't want it to cause further harm to an already suffering church. However, after much discernment, Jesus led me to write about this experience with the hope of it helping others who had suffered similarly or had walked away from the church injured. In addition, this taught me invaluable spiritual lessons that allowed me to grow stronger in my faith and more in love with the Catholic Church, despite the sinfulness and brokenness of some of its members or leaders. We will never grow or take steps towards healing if we are not willing to first acknowledge the problems and then expose them to the light of Christ to remediate them appropriately and expeditiously.

As I previously mentioned, Fr. Ben who invited me to minister in his parish was a friend of mine. I highly respected and admired him, not to mention, he was extremely gifted and I trusted him. I had met him years earlier during inner-healing conferences in that state. He was very active with the youth and young adults, who later became his close friends. He shared with me that he was having problems with one of the young men who had become rebellious and very unappreciative and thus wanted me to help him. To protect his identity, I will call him "David." Fr. Ben painted such a negative picture of David that I didn't know what to expect. To my surprise, when I met this 20-year-old man, he was extremely nice, helpful and transparent. I was cautious with him initially, due to what Fr. Ben had told me about him, and I was concerned about being manipulated.

My friend Lourdes had driven with me from Sacramento to accompany me on the long trip and help me settle into my new place. She was also involved in the inner-healing ministry and was a friend of Fr. Ben as well. Upon our arrival, Fr. Ben requested Lourdes to pray with some of the young men who were close to him and worked for the church. Since Lourdes was leaving a few days later and I was staying for the year, Fr. Ben felt these young men might open up more to her because they wouldn't see her again.

I remember clearly the day she prayed in private with David. Usually a prayer session lasted 60 to 90 minutes. However, Lourdes spent four hours with him. When she came out she had a startled pale look on her face and I knew there was something very wrong. Lourdes told me that David had given her permission to share with me what he told her because she was leaving town soon and I needed to be informed.

As Lourdes started recounting David's story, I felt the world around me collapsing. I wanted it all to be just a bad nightmare. David had very legitimate reasons to be rebellious with Fr. Ben. He felt trapped by him. When David had first met him, David was alone in this country, spoke very little English, and had limited financial means. Fr. Ben took an interest in him, giving him moral and even monetary support. David trusted Fr. Ben as a spiritual father and a friend. Although David didn't have the means to go to college, Fr. Ben told him he received funds from wealthy families to support youth without financial means. He offered to pay for his tuition and help him daily at the rectory with his English classes. He also employed David at the church.

Initially, David was very grateful for Fr. Ben's care and support and trusted him. However, with the passage of time, he started feeling uncomfortable by Fr. Ben's behavior. On many occasions after helping David with his studies, Fr. Ben would ask David to give him a back massage because he felt so tired. Eventually, this evolved into a body massage, often fully naked. With time, things progressed into more sexual fondling. David felt very trapped and uneasy. He bluntly told Fr. Ben that he didn't like these acts and wasn't a homosexual. Fr. Ben became very manipulative and accused David of overreacting and misreading things, assuring him that he wasn't homosexual either. He became very controlling and quick tempered with David. He tried to manipulate David by lavishing him with material gifts, sending money to his parents in Mexico and even taking him on a vacation to Europe. David felt he was sinking in a deep hole and didn't know how to get out of it. He felt overpowered by this priest and had no one to turn to for help. Fr. Ben was so well known and respected in the

15

community because of his position and charisma, David knew that nobody would believe his story. He prayed very hard for God to rescue him from this dreadful situation. He felt that Lourdes and I were God's response to his desperate plea! It seemed that David wasn't the only one suffering like this. He alluded to other young men who were equally manipulated into similar situations.

When Lourdes finished telling me David's story, I felt like screaming. I knew in my heart that he was telling the truth. There were some details in his story that matched exactly a story I heard previously from another young man. He knew this priest from a youth conference and questioned Fr. Ben's behavior during a visit to him. Out of my friendship and deep respect for Fr. Ben, I questioned the youth's story. I saw how gifted Fr. Ben was and naïvely believed he was incapable of such behavior. However, the details of his story remained in the back of my mind as a red flag.

That night I could not sleep. I felt so hurt, betrayed and manipulated by my friend Fr. Ben and so outraged for David and other helpless victims like him. They all had similar profiles, barely over 18, Mexican citizens, spoke limited English and needed financial and moral support. I was convinced that the reason Fr. Ben invited me to his parish was to help "fix" David as he was the only victim who had the courage to stand against him. Fr. Ben knew how much I trusted him; he mistakenly thought he could continue to manipulate me with his lies.

That weekend, when Lourdes was about to return to Sacramento, I went into the chapel in the convent where I lived, to complain to the Lord Jesus. I expressed to Him my deep agony and grief about the entire situation, how betrayed I felt and how I thought I wasn't the right person to deal with this predicament. I wished to return to Sacramento with Lourdes that same day as it was just too painful for me. Suddenly, I heard deep in my soul Jesus' response: *"You told me about your pain. Now you will feel Mine!"*

Instantly, I started experiencing excruciating internal pain. I started sobbing uncontrollably for an entire hour. My agony was so deep that it was only God's grace that sustained me. When the pain finally stopped, Jesus said to me: *"Now that you have experienced My pain, will you still abandon Me?"* I started weeping and asking Jesus for forgiveness for my selfishness. I was so focused on my own pain and had forgotten that it was Jesus who was suffering the most. He was being betrayed, scourged and crucified again by the grievous sins of one of His beloved chosen ones, beloved like Judas, one of His 12 apostles, who used his free will to betray Jesus and sell Him for 30 pieces of silver. Jesus had entrusted Fr. Ben with the protection and spiritual guidance of His innocent children! The harm committed against them was scourging Jesus all over again. Jesus assured me that He chose me and prepared me for this mission. The key was to remain united to Him always, and I needed to take time off to be in deep prayer daily. Jesus made it clear to me that I needed to start my day with daily Mass, unite myself to Him through His Word and the Eucharist, and also spend three hours in Eucharistic Adoration prayer before ministering to others.

Jesus taught me that if He sent me on a mission, no matter how difficult, He would give me everything I needed to accomplish it. It wasn't about what I could do, but what He could accomplish through me as His instrument, acting through my willingness and surrender. The key was to always remain focused on Him and not on myself. I was reminded of Peter walking on water. As long as he kept his eyes focused on Jesus, he was able to defy natural laws, but once Peter took his eyes off the Lord and looked at himself and his own limited capacities, he started sinking.

I felt strengthened by Jesus' instructions and decided to stay to fulfill the mission. I spoke with David who shared his story with me and provided me with names of potential other victims. He did not give me permission to talk to Fr. Ben yet about what he shared with me because he was afraid of retaliation and losing his opportunity to go to college. David asked me to wait until he was emotionally ready for the next step. He was grateful for my support as he knew he was no longer alone.

In many ways, I felt my hands were completely tied. David was not a minor for me to report Fr. Ben to the police; he was 20 years old and was considered an adult. His communication with me was also confidential and I needed his consent to talk to Fr. Ben about the accusations. I couldn't report Fr. Ben to his diocese to initiate an investigation without David's approval and corroboration. The only thing I could do was to remain prayerful about the situation awaiting God's instructions.

As hard as it was for me to be normal with Fr. Ben after all that I learned, I knew I needed to remain always in a place of love. I wasn't there to judge or prosecute anyone. God sent me there to bring inner healing to those involved and accomplish His will. I prayed and asked Jesus to give me His peace so that I would be able to discern His will always. I could tell that Fr. Ben became more nervous with me, and he began probing me with many questions, trying to see if David told me anything, while continuing to speak negatively of him. He got very irritated with me when I defended David and didn't like it when he saw me spending time with him.

Working daily and closely with this priest allowed me to see how different he was from the charismatic person I knew from the conferences or as a friend. He was very controlling, manipulative, short tempered and always tense, which made everyone around him fearful of him in the parish office. I offered to pray with him several times for the healing of his childhood wounds, but to no avail. His behavior reflected his deep brokenness. I knew from experience that if he sincerely opened his heart to Jesus' healing love and liberating truth, he could be healed from the root of the emotional wounds that were causing his ungodly behavior.

People tend to forget that priests are also human like the rest of us. Many grew up in dysfunctional families suffering various emotional wounds—such as physical, emotional or sexual abuse, abandonment, rejection, bullying, divorce, alcoholic or violent parents—and need inner healing. It is impossible to live in this world and not have it affect us negatively in one way or another, regardless of our vocation or status in life. Getting emotionally wounded is a natural by-product of being alive in a fallen world populated by imperfect, sinful humanity. It is a certainty that our heart will be emotionally hurt along the way. It takes tremendous courage to face our past, especially the childhood memories that we struggle hard to forget or block.

I was introduced to the parishioners at the weekend Masses where I spoke about my inner-healing prayer ministry that was available to them through the kindness of the parish. Within a short period of time, many parishioners started coming to me for individual inner-healing prayer sessions, and my calendar filled up quickly. Out of ignorance, I started reducing my personal 3-hour prayer time to be able to serve more people. My prayer time was eventually reduced to 10 minutes after Mass instead of the three hours that the Lord Jesus required of me. Within a few weeks, I noticed that I became easily irritable, short tempered and very exhausted. I couldn't understand what was happening with me and I felt like a failure. I even considered ending my mission early to return to California.

After Mass one day, I went into deep prayer to discern God's will. Jesus spoke clearly to my heart showing me that the reason I felt so depleted and irritable was because I had stopped spending quality prayer time with Him. He added that if my day was too busy to afford me the hours of prayer He required of me, that meant I had things on my calendar that were not from Him. Jesus taught me that many well-intentioned people made the mistake of serving God without spending time with Him. Thus, they became an easy prey for the demonic spirits who battled them in their weariness and human weakness. That was why the prayer time I spent with Jesus daily was non-negotiable. It was His time to instruct, direct, refuel, strengthen and refresh me. I had no strength on my own to engage in intense spiritual work and warfare unless I was first united to Him by prayer. This was an invaluable lesson that helped me to withstand all the persecutions that followed and to accomplish my mission there. The lesson also prepared me for my international missionary work and even my devastating illnesses.

Within a few months, it became clear to Fr. Ben that David had shared his story with me. He told me that he expected me to be his ally and friend and felt betrayed that I was siding with David. I told him that I sided only with the truth, reminding him that as a missionary my main employer was Jesus; I was accountable to Him. I quickly became viewed as a threat by Fr. Ben, but by then, my ministry had flourished in the parish. Parishioners were thanking him for bringing me there, so even if he contemplated terminating my missionary work early, he would have had a hard time explaining it to the community. In an attempt to have me leave on my own, he started persecuting me in the most painful ways possible and in the last place I ever imagined!

For me, attending daily Mass was the most sacred and important part of my day. I hadn't missed a daily Mass since 2002. In Mass, I felt God's presence the most, and when I received the Eucharist, I knew I was receiving Jesus in His Body, Blood, Soul and Divinity. Nothing on earth was more important to me than that and at Mass, I felt safe and at "home" spiritually. Fr. Ben knew how important the Eucharist and Mass were to me. He started attacking me during his daily homilies. He never said my name directly, but it became clear to me and to other people attending Mass that I was the subject of his homily. I often would close my eyes and ask Jesus to give me His graces to persevere even though I felt like crying or walking out. I couldn't fathom how it was possible that I could be persecuted in such a holy place, in the house of God and by one of His chosen ones. My pain was unbearable but I kept my eyes focused on Jesus, and He continued to sustain me. I wished I could attend another Catholic Church for daily Mass, but unfortunately this was the only church in that small town.

When Fr. Ben saw that his verbal attacks were not working, he tried to attack me where it would hurt the most. One day, as I went up for Communion to receive the Eucharist as usual, instead of placing the Host on my tongue as expected, He placed his hand on my head to give me a blessing. At first, I was too stunned to comprehend his gesture, so I reopened my mouth to receive the Eucharist. He shook his head gesturing that he was denying me Communion. As I walked away in shock and about to burst into tears, I heard Jesus' voice resounding deeply within my heart saying: "*Offer Me now the sacrifice and pain of not being able to receive Me in the Eucharist for his repentance and conversion. You cannot offer Me anything greater than that, not even your own life.*" Such powerful words and teaching! He was absolutely right. Nothing and nobody is greater than Jesus in the Eucharist. This was the greatest sacrifice I could offer up for Fr. Ben, and when I obeyed Jesus right away my spirit was flooded with peace replacing all the pain.

It never ceased to amaze me how much Jesus loves us, no matter how sinful we were or how much we offended Him. He showed me clearly how I could quickly turn something evil intended to cause me harm into something good. Only God could bring goodness out of any evil if we offered it to Him with open loving hearts.

Unfortunately the persecutions did not stop there. Fr. Ben turned several parish employees against me; he had such a way of manipulating things to make it appear he was the victim. I kept on offering my daily pain and suffering to Jesus as He taught me. I was there to fulfill a mission no matter how painful or difficult it was. Jesus was my strength and I kept my eyes focused only on Him.

David and I became very good friends through our prayer time together. The Lord Jesus used me to restore his faith and hope in God, in spite of what he had endured. David finally warned Fr. Ben that if he didn't stop hurting other young men with his inappropriate sexual behavior, David was going to take action against him. Fr. Ben laughed it off because he knew David had too much to lose if he did, especially his college education.

I prayed a lot with David for his healing and to be able to discern God's will. When David found out that Fr. Ben was continuing his behavior, he decided to move forward to file a complaint with the local diocese to stop the abuse. Initially, none of the other victims that I had also prayed with had the courage to join David but two more joined in later. I promised David to support him with the entire process. We met with the diocesan investigator outside of town and initiated the investigation. I told the diocese everything I knew and what I had gone through, and I also gave them the names of all the other victims known to me.

Meanwhile, Fr. Ben sensed there was something happening. In his final desperate attempt to get rid of me quickly, he asked to meet with me and told me he had run out of funds to pay for my monthly stipend. Instead, he had a gift for me, an airline ticket for me to go on a pilgrimage alone to Medjugorje for two weeks. He clearly knew how much I loved Medjugorje and thought I would never refuse such an offer. However, my departure city was San Francisco, California. He suggested that I terminate my missionary work much earlier than we had agreed upon and return to California in preparation for my trip. I smiled and thanked him while my heart was bleeding on the inside. I felt such deep sadness for Fr. Ben. He had so many opportunities to change his ways, to repent and even to avail himself of my prayer ministry. Unfortunately, he used his free will to stay in the darkness. His attempt to bribe me completely failed and I immediately forwarded the itinerary of the purchased airline ticket to the diocesan investigator as further proof of how Fr. Ben tried to lure people monetarily to achieve his goals.

Within 10 days, the diocese completed the investigation. He was removed from the parish and sent to a treatment center for five months. The parishioners were never told the truth concerning the reasons behind his removal, which really upset me and all the victims. The local bishop and the parochial vicar (second priest at the parish) asked me to stay in the parish for two more months to help with the healing process. Amazingly, a beautiful generous family who appreciated my ministry made a donation to pay my full stipend for the two remaining months.

Despite everything I suffered, my faith in Jesus never wavered. Even though Jesus is the Head of the Church, we as members of His Mystical Body on earth, still struggle against the sinful fallen world and the flesh. He gave each of us a free will to choose to live according to His commandments or to disobey them. St. Peter taught us: *"Be sober, be watchful. Your adversary the devil prowls around like a roaring lion, seeking someone to devour."* (1 Peter 5:8). The key to resist the attacks of the enemy or his temptations is to stay united to Jesus through prayer. As previously mentioned, Jesus was betrayed by His apostle Judas. Even Peter denied Him three times, but at least he fully repented and gave his life by dying for Jesus and His Church. Despite my painful experience with Fr. Ben, I knew he didn't reflect the entire Church. He made his sinful choices and would have to answer to Jesus one day. I continue to pray for his repentance, inner healing and conversion.

Over the years, I have met many dedicated virtuous priests who serve others selflessly and are men with deep prayer lives. I learned from my experience never to put any human on a pedestal, regardless of his or her title or position in life. As long as we have a will, we are capable of sinning and causing harm to others. We have a choice to be instruments of God or instruments of his enemy, the devil. We need to remain prayerful, pray for each other, remaining humble with our eyes always fixed on the sinless One, Jesus.

In addition to all the spiritual lessons, I was very grateful to God for all the wonderful friends I met! They became a spiritual family providing me with much support, love and wonderful memories, especially during the difficult periods.

Another great blessing to me was that God chose that state to be the first place to market my first book. Many of the people who benefitted from my ministry were anxiously awaiting its publication. Some had read the manuscript and were so deeply touched that they told others about it. One of these people was Andrea who later became a very close friend. She was able to relate to my story and return to God for a relationship she had been longing for, but felt unworthy of having. Reading the manuscript brought her closer to God. Overnight, her life changed and she began going to Daily Mass and fell in love with Jesus! When Andrea's mom saw the sudden change in her daughter, she became intrigued and wanted to read it. However, her primary language was Spanish and my book was only written in English then. She approached her close friend Raquel, who happened to be fully bilingual and a Spanish professor at the local college, hoping she would translate it for her. Raquel read the manuscript and loved it. She shared it with her brother Enrique who was equally very touched by it. They both felt that the book would greatly benefit the Spanish-speaking community bringing much needed inner healing. Despite their very busy lives, they offered to translate the book into Spanish, completely free of charge as I had no money to pay them. They completed the task with so much love and sacrifice. I will be eternally grateful to them.

I was so overwhelmed by God's love and marveled to witness the unfolding of His divine plan. I saw clearly how He moved the heart of each person to accomplish His will, as if each one of us was a piece of a jigsaw puzzle, each equally important to complete God's marvelous picture.

In February 2009, I was able to find a great self-publishing company that agreed to publish my book in English and Spanish. It was exactly 30 days from the day I contacted them to the day my book was published and up for sale online at Amazon and other sites——the same number of days it took me to write the book.

Jesus had previously told me that He would provide for all my needs and I should never worry about any of the details. I just needed to attend to His affairs and He would take care of mine! I saw God's grace and power in every aspect of my life. Each day, my faith grew stronger. With every breath, I was more in love with my Lord Jesus.

Chapter 5

Inner-Healing Prayer Ministry

"Then Jesus went about all the cities and villages, teaching in their synagogues, and proclaiming the good news of the kingdom, and curing every disease and every sickness." — Matt. 9:35

I felt a great sense of relief upon returning to Sacramento in June 2009, since I needed to recover from my intense mission experience. Unfortunately, one week before departing for home, I was playing basketball with some friends from the parish, and I fell and tore a ligament in my left ankle. I had played three sports throughout high school and had various ankle injuries that always healed with no problem. However, this time my ankle only got worse with time, affecting my gait and the rest of my body. Unbeknownst to me, the ankle injury was not the primary problem. The fall resulted from one of my diseases that were not correctly diagnosed until two years later in 2011 which I will discuss more thoroughly in a later chapter. Meanwhile, I offered my ankle pain to God for the healing of the Church, especially after my mission experience.

Upon my return home, many people contacted me for individual inner-healing prayer sessions. At the time, I prayed with them at the side chapel inside Immaculate Conception Church, which was not always convenient due to frequent interruptions. I prayed to Jesus asking for a private office, not knowing how I would be able to afford it. Within a few days, Deacon Jerry, the administrator of Immaculate Conception Church at the time, approached me with an offer of an office, rent-free, at the parish. Deacon Jerry was a very strong advocate of my ministry as he had seen its fruits in the lives of youth and adults from prior years. He knew I was providing a valuable ministry at no charge to local and non-local parishioners and wanted to support me. Of course, I gratefully accepted donations from people to enable me to pay for my living expenses and monthly bills.

Words were insufficient to express my gratitude to Jesus for always providing for my needs. All I needed to do was to remain in His will and be prayerful, trusting and patient. I told Jesus in prayer that I was willing to do whatever He would ask of me to serve Him. To ensure that it wasn't me or my ego initiating things, I waited as Jesus brought the tasks to me. I didn't want to jump ahead of God, like I had often done in the past and if He wanted me to pray with His children, I knew Jesus would bring them to me. If He wished for me to speak somewhere like I had done prior to my mission, I needed to be invited to do so. Within a few weeks, word spread quickly in both the English-and Spanish-speaking communities about my return to California and the availability of my ministry. I started receiving invitations to speak at Catholic conferences, retreats and prayer groups throughout California, other states and Mexico. Between 2009 and 2012, I gave over 300 talks! In addition, my calendar quickly filled up with people seeking inner healing for themselves or their willing family members. Some people did not have the financial means to go to secular psychologists, while others were looking for healing through Christ because secular therapy never healed the root of their spiritual and emotional suffering.

As human beings, we're made up of physical material, the body, which can be seen and touched. We're also made up of immaterial aspects, which are intangible——this includes the soul, spirit, intellect, will, emotions and conscience. These immaterial characteristics exist beyond the physical lifespan of the human body and are therefore eternal. Genesis 2:7 states that man was created as a "living soul." The soul consists of the mind (which includes the conscience), the will, and the emotions. The soul and the spirit are tied together and make up what the Scriptures call the "heart," where the Holy Spirit dwells. These immaterial aspects——the spirit, soul, heart, conscience, mind and emotions——make up the whole personality. The Bible makes it clear that the soul and spirit are the primary immaterial aspects of humanity, while the body is the physical container that holds them on this earth. Just as the physical body gets wounded and infected through cuts or injuries, also our spirit and soul get wounded through childhood painful events or trauma which fill with lies, shame, anger, anxiety, fear, unforgivingness and other toxins——that require Jesus' healing.

Jesus wants to heal us of the damages we may have to our soul. For some He has permitted the damage because He would not interfere with the human will of those who inflicted the pain. However, He wants to heal us from the consequences of it and can liberate us from our lies and heal all our wounds. The Lord Jesus stated that to us when He read the words of the prophet Isaiah that were fulfilled in Him: *"The Spirit of the Lord is upon me, because he has anointed me to bring glad tidings to the poor. He has sent me to proclaim liberty to captives and recovery of sight to the blind, to let the oppressed go free, and to proclaim a year acceptable to the Lord."* (Luke 4:18–19)

Jesus came to bring all of us, regardless of our differences, the good news that He is still alive today. He is here to liberate us from the bondage of Satan's lies and restore our "sight"——our physical, emotional and spiritual sight. He wants us to be "free" from our "oppression" which is causing many people in today's world to be severely depressed and filled with despair and hopelessness. Some depend on one or more anti-depression pills to survive each day. This is Jesus' time to bring the joy and freedom back to our souls and hearts. He clearly stated *"...I came so that they might have life and have it more abundantly."* (John 10:10). Yes, Jesus wants us to live life in abundance. I do not believe He is referring particularly to "financial" abundance here. Jesus was poor Himself and never sought money, luxury or fame in His life. Jesus was humble and simple in

His ways. He came to give us the Good News of love, forgiveness, mercy, healing and freedom.

The reality is that most people——regardless of their ethnic, social or economic backgrounds——live in emotional pain, whether they acknowledge it or not. Let's look at some of the common *symptoms* of emotional wounds in our own lives, our families or in the world around us:

- Addictions: As a result of false beliefs about ourselves, usually rooted in our childhood that continue to cause inner turmoil, it's easy to want to numb our feelings or escape our pain or reality. This can be in the form of excessive drinking, recreational or prescription drug abuse, overeating, smoking, gambling, pornography, sex addictions, spending binges, workaholism, etc. Unfortunately, addictions open the door for "spirits of addiction" to enter into our souls, which makes them much harder to fight with our own human strength.

- Feelings of worthlessness or unworthiness: Often some people grow up without love or bonding with one or both of their parents, while others grow up in abusive or alcoholic families, where there is no real love or protection. In either case, we can swallow the lies that we are worthless or unworthy, believing there is something wrong with us.

- Self-hatred or self-blame: Many times if we suffered from childhood abuse, we begin to think that perhaps what happened to us was deserved because of something we did or the way that we were.

- Irritability: It's easy to become irritable with others, even if they aren't doing anything wrong.

- Little or no tolerance: There's a low tolerance level with others in what we expect and demand from them.

- Negative feelings always rising up: Feeling of anger, hate, resentment, etc., seem to "rise up" within us at the slightest offense from others.

- Overly sensitive about an event in our past: If there are events in our past which cause us to become very sensitive or angry, or even cause us to lash out, then it's likely revealing a deep emotional wound or false beliefs tied to that event or memory.

- Hard to feel loved: It's hard to clearly see or accept the love of others and God in our life. We may be surrounded by people who love us, but it can be difficult to fully feel and receive that love. There seems to be a wall up that blocks the flow of love into our life.

- Lashing out: When there's an inner wound that has festered, it becomes easy to lash out or have sudden outbursts of anger, hate, resentment, etc. We may find it easy to lash out at people who love us and have done us no harm.

- Hard to forgive: It becomes very difficult, if not impossible to love and therefore forgive others. It can also be hard to forgive and love ourselves.

- Feelings of anger towards God: When we have been wounded, especially abused, rejected or abandoned, by our own father or mother, it becomes easy to project onto God our pain and anger. Our image of God is often formed by our image of our earthly fathers. Many of us blame God for our troubles and hardships. This is the last thing that we want to do when seeking to be healed, because it virtually puts a wall in our mind and hearts that can block the healing power of the Holy Spirit to operate. Although God desires to heal our wounds, He will not violate our free will, and if we hold hate in our heart against Him, it can block His efforts to heal our wounds.

- Hard to trust others: We learn trust in our childhood. If our parents love us, protect us and provide for us, we will learn to trust. When our trust is broken or violated in our childhood, we quickly learn that it's not safe to trust others, including God.

In the inner-healing process, the struggles in our present lives are often found to be rooted in early experiences in our childhood or even as far back as the womb. Many of us have been wounded even in the womb. Our spirit was formed by God from the moment we were conceived in our mother's womb, and whatever emotions our mothers felt during the nine months of pregnancy, we also felt them. If the pregnancy was not welcomed or if there were discussions or attempts to abort the baby, our spirit felt the fear, anxiety and the rejection of our mother. I prayed often with adults who were suicidal or believed their life was worthless. Some suffered from depression or severe anxiety. During the prayer time, the Lord Jesus often revealed to the person that the root of their suicidal thoughts or their anxiety stemmed from lies believed in the womb. Some believed they didn't deserve to live, were unwanted or were a mistake. Even though the mother never had the abortion, the lies or fears swallowed back in the womb remained and manifested throughout their adulthood.

My inner-healing prayer ministry is centered on healing through Jesus Christ. Jesus *is* Love. His Divine Love is the perfect medicine for all the wounds of the soul. As humans, God created us out of love and His original plan was that we would be born into this world as the fruit of the love of our mother and father. The love of both is crucial for our emotional and spiritual formation and well-being. A mother's love alone does not compensate for the love of an absent father, nor does the love of a father alone compensate for the love of an absent mother. We need the healthy love and protection of both. Let's reflect on Jesus' example. Even though Mary did not require a man for His conception, since He was conceived by the Holy Spirit, our Heavenly Father brought St. Joseph into His life to be His earthly father, to protect and love Him, and to teach Him how to become a man. Whenever we lack the love of either parent or believe in our minds that we are not loved by one or both of them, we become severely wounded directly in our souls. When events or circumstances occur in our childhood that lead us to believe we are unloved or even unlovable, we develop huge wounds in our souls that get infected with the devil's lies. These lies affect us for most of our lives unless we open our hearts to receive Jesus' divine healing love and liberating truth. We usually project these wounds directly on to God, especially if we believe that our own earthly father who is visible to us does not love us. If so, this makes it more difficult to believe in the love of our invisible Heavenly Father.

Jesus *is* Truth, and the Truth sets us free (John 14:6, 8:32). In the prayer session, I encourage the person to discover and expose what he or she believes is a falsehood. Then, I encourage him/her to have an encounter with Jesus Christ through prayer, thus allowing the Lord to reveal His Truth to the wounded person's heart and mind. It is not about giving advice, diagnosing problems, or sharing opinions or insight. It is about allowing a person to have a personal encounter with the Lord Jesus in the midst of the person's emotional pain, setting him/her free.

I noticed through my prayer sessions with the hundreds (or even thousands) of people I have prayed with since 2001, patterns of common emotional wounds that affect many people. With the hope of bringing some healing to some of my readers, I'd like to share one story that illustrates the depth of these wounds.

A concerned mother brought her 16 year-old son to my office. I'll call him "Joe." Joe was drinking a lot, smoking pot and didn't want to go to Mass. He was very angry with God. When he sat in my office, it became evident to me that he was there against his will and he looked furious. I told him that I only could help people who are willing to be helped as Jesus would never violate his free will during the prayer session. I added that he could leave if he wanted, but I could tell he had deep pain. Joe responded angrily that he hated God and didn't want to have anything to do with Him. I replied that he had the right to feel what he felt, however, I wanted to know why he hated God so much. He quickly responded: "*Where was your God when my father abandoned me and my mother at the age of two. Why did he allow him to go and form a different family with other children, forgetting completely about me all these years?*"

I told him that even though I could answer his question, I wanted him to hear the response directly from Jesus, if he was willing. He nodded in approval. I asked him to close his eyes to try to disconnect from the physical world and turn inward inside his heart to hear Jesus' response. I addressed Jesus reiterating Joe's same question. As I was observing Joe's angry face, I noticed his cheeks started to tremble as a few tears flowed from his eyes. I asked him what Jesus responded. Joe replied: "*Jesus said that it was never His will that my father abandon me and my mom. My dad is a grown up man and has a free will. Jesus would not violate his will.*" I asked Joe to stay in his heart connected to Jesus and I asked Jesus where He was when Joe's dad abandoned him. Then I asked Jesus if He too had abandoned him. Within a few minutes, I saw Joe's body curl up in the chair and he started sobbing heavily for a while. I knew something transcendent was happening within him and I waited until he was ready to talk. When I asked him what had just happened, he said that he felt like Jesus was embracing him. Joe felt heat and love in his entire body as he heard Jesus tell him: "*I never abandoned you and will never do so. I have always been with you and suffered your pain with you.*" We prayed more during the session, allowing Jesus to speak more truth to Joe. An hour later, Joe left my office a transformed person. He had a personal encounter with Jesus who, through His liberating truth and love, brought healing to Joe's deepest wounds. A few weeks later, his mother told me that Joe became more pleasant and confident and had stopped smoking marijuana and drinking. He went to confession and started attending Mass on Sundays. His life changed dramatically after Jesus started healing his heart.

We live in a generation where many people, like Joe, are growing up with a deep fatherly wound. Some have been abandoned by their fathers; others grew up with an emotionally absent father, or an abusive or alcoholic one. Some fathers provide for their children's material needs, but they are absent when the time comes to satisfy the needs of the heart, such as intimacy and connection. Most of these fathers had never bonded with their own fathers and repeat the cycle with their own children. In all these situations, the children develop deep emotional wounds. I notice many boys grow up feeling inadequate with a deep void in their soul. Many resort to addictive behaviors in an attempt to fill the hole in their heart or avoid the pain. So many boys do not have a father affirming their leap into manhood, and their transition is often filled with feelings of fear, anger and frustration, instead of confidence and security. For girls who lack bonding with their fathers, many later on try to fill the void in their hearts by seeking love from any man who would give them any attention. Unfortunately, many end up feeling emptier and very hurt emotionally.

Another very common childhood wound is sexual abuse. I have prayed with and talked to many adults, men and women from all walks of life and cultures, who were innocent victims of this horrendous act. The numbers in both genders are very high, especially in the male population. Unfortunately, the shame attached to male child sexual abuse is even greater than that for a female. Instead of being an advocate for the innocent male victims, society tends to shame them more by bringing their masculinity into question. The lives of both men and women victims are severely affected. The consequences range widely: many have intimacy problems as adults, many become sexually promiscuous in their early teens, many become confused about their sexual orientation, many victims become perpetrators themselves and sexually abuse other innocent children, many try to numb their pain through severe addictions to alcohol, drugs, sex, pornography, food, cigarettes, gambling, shopping or even work, and many block the memories completely, denying the sexual abuse ever occurred in order to be able to survive. The shame, guilt and the lies that are internalized are often overwhelming. This is such a deplorable crime which occurs repeatedly in our world, but many people are too ashamed to confront it or discuss it!

I have had the great privilege during the prayer sessions with sexual abuse victims to witness Jesus liberate many women and men from all the shame, guilt, self-blame, fear, anxiety, depression, anger and lies that they had carried since their childhood. Many later told me that their lives were completely transformed. In many situations, Jesus accomplished in one hour what many years of secular therapy couldn't. Jesus restored lasting peace to their hearts through His healing love and liberating truth. Victims heard Jesus telling them in their hearts: *"It wasn't your fault. You were an innocent victim. You are clean. You are worthy. You didn't lose your value. You are precious. I love you."*

Indeed, Jesus is the Truth and He sets the captives free!

Chapter 6

Missions to Mexico

"I can do all things through Him who strengthens me." — Phil. 4:13

As I was growing up, I never considered learning Spanish. I spoke my native language, Arabic, and had been learning English and French since I was four years old in Jordan. However, God's plan for my life was greater than anything I could ever conceive on my own.

In 1990, after a year studying abroad in France and my visit to Medjugorje, I returned to UC Davis to continue my university education. I felt the Lord Jesus was urging me to learn Spanish. At that time I shared an apartment with my dear friend Andrea, who was half Argentinian and spoke Spanish fluently. I didn't speak a word of Spanish then. Andrea had many friends who came from all over Latin America to work on their graduate level degrees. I became close friends with them and we often ate lunch together. They invited me to go out on the weekends to dance clubs where "Salsa" and "Merengue" styles of dancing were popular. I loved how my friends danced with each other to this wonderful Caribbean beat, and I resolved to learn how to dance like them. In fact, dancing became my escape from all the university-related pressures.

The more time I spent with my Latino friends, the more I realized it was crucial for me to learn Spanish in order for our friendship to deepen. They spoke only Spanish to each other when I was around them. Although they often translated what they were saying, I knew that I only received the general idea of the conversation. They seemed to be having a great time, and I wanted to participate in the discussions. They were not trying to be rude or inconsiderate; they were just more comfortable speaking in their native tongue.

I realized that it would be fairly easy for me to learn Spanish since it was very similar to French, with the exception of the pronunciation. In fact, Spanish was actually much easier to pronounce than French. Thus, during my final year at UC Davis, I enrolled in and completed one full year of Spanish courses. I was not afraid to speak or make mistakes, so I immersed myself into the rich Latino culture by listening to Spanish radio, watching Spanish television (particularly Mexican soap operas), and of course, practicing Spanish with my friends. Before too long, I became fluent in the language.

I was very grateful to my friends for all the ways they blessed and enriched my journey in life. I learned so much from them about their beautiful cultures and countries that university books could never teach me. Unbeknownst to them, they were preparing me for an essential part of my spiritual growth and my inner-healing prayer ministry to thousands of Spanish-speaking people in the United States and abroad, especially in Mexico.

At the end of 2009, I received a call from Teo and Juanita, a wonderful and faith-filled Mexican-American couple that I had first met in 2007, after I gave my testimony in Spanish to about 15,000 young people at the Los Angeles Sports Arena. They had been touched by what I shared and they contacted me after the event. Since then we have become very close friends. When they called me this time, it was to invite me to speak at a three-day Catholic retreat, known as "*Kerygma*," in their hometown in Mexico. Juanita had previously gifted the organizers with my first book and after reading it, they had requested that I participate as a speaker at the retreat. They graciously invited me to stay with Juanita's family.

As soon as I arrived at Juanita's house, I immediately felt at home. Her beautiful mother and all 10 siblings, along with their families, welcomed me into their hearts and homes with open, loving arms. They even adopted me as an additional sister and called me *"carnala,"* which is a word of endearment in Spanish signifying a "blood sister." They were God's faithful instruments in fulfilling His plan during all my missions in Mexico. They helped me, protected me, drove me to conferences in various states, and provided for all my needs and more. We worked together in perfect harmony as a team, as if we had known each other all our lives. They truly became like my second family, and I was grateful to God for blessing me with their friendship, unconditional love and generosity!

At the *Kerygma* retreat, I was amazed by the openness of the hearts of the 300 people who attended. They stayed at the retreat center overnight for the three days, and the Lord Jesus manifested His love, powerfully transforming their hearts. I gave many talks during the retreat and prayed extensively for their inner healing each day. One of the other speakers was a priest and was touched by my talks. He invited me to return to Mexico the following month to speak at a weekend retreat in his parish in La Piedad, Michoacan, and I gladly accepted.

I was amazed to see, once again, God's marvelous plan unfolding in my life! Not only did I return the following month in February of 2010, I also returned for five full weeks in July of 2010, four weeks in January of 2011 and five more weeks in July of 2011. I had more trips planned in 2012 to Mexico and Guatemala but was forced to cancel due to the rapid progression of the illnesses that left me fully paralyzed. My doctors advised me to stop traveling since it became too dangerous for someone in my condition.

During my trip in July 2010, word spread fast in the surrounding towns and cities that I was back. My calendar filled up quickly and at one point I was invited to speak in a different place each day for thirty consecutive days. This took me to four different states: Guanajuato, Jalisco, Michoacan and San Luis Potosí.

I faced many health-related challenges during this mission. Upon my arrival in Mexico, both of my ankles were extremely swollen and remained so for the entire trip. I was having difficulty walking and kept falling. I ended up going to Morelia, Michoacan to obtain Magnetic Resonance Imaging (MRI) for both ankles. The results indicated I had torn ligaments from old injuries and had much swelling (edema) in both. Looking back, I know now that multiple sclerosis was already progressing in my body and affecting me on many different levels. I hadn't been diagnosed yet and assumed that all my physical problems resulted from my ankle issues. I had such a busy agenda every day and had developed a high tolerance to pain. I tried to ignore the pain and discomfort, and focused on doing God's work.

Another health challenge began two weeks after my arrival; I started having symptoms of a bad cold and a painful cough. I went to the doctor and he gave me some medication so I wouldn't have to cancel any of my speaking engagements so I continued with my missions. One Saturday, I woke up without a voice and I could only whisper, but I was scheduled to speak at a day-long retreat in Pastor Ortiz, Michoacan. I always started my days with Mass at 6:00 AM before I spoke anywhere in Mexico, and after I received the Eucharist that day, I went back to my pew, knelt down and spoke to Jesus in my heart. I told him that I had no voice and didn't know how I was going to give two talks that day. I was supposed to share my testimony, followed by a talk on inner healing and then with prayers. Jesus spoke to my heart clearly saying: "*Do not worry. Everything will be fine. I am glorified in your nothingness.*" His words comforted me. He was reminding me that I was only His instrument. On my own, I was nothing. His will was accomplished through my surrender and willingness, regardless of my limitations. It wasn't about my abilities, but what He could accomplish through me. I knew He was going to do something powerful, so I just trusted in Him and obeyed.

I went to the retreat with Juanita, her sister Chayo and her husband Teo. Chayo quickly became a close friend and my right-hand person during all my missions in Mexico. She was very concerned about me and how I was going to give my talks. She suggested I alert the priest in charge about my voice-problem. I approached the priest and whispered to him that I had laryngitis and had lost my voice. He had a very worried look on his face but I assured him that our Lord Jesus was going to manifest powerfully despite my limitations. I asked him if I could give my two talks back to back since my testimony and inner-healing talk were connected. I also asked him if it was possible to expose the Blessed Sacrament during my talk. My testimony was centered on Jesus and He was the Healer who transformed my life. The priest confirmed to me he felt the prompting of the Holy Spirit to trust and move forward with these requests considering my condition.

Before I started sharing my testimony and inner-healing prayers, I prostrated myself before the Blessed Sacrament and said to Jesus: "*My Lord, I give You my nothingness. Be glorified!*" As I held the microphone to start my talk with my usual opening prayer, a miracle took place that was witnessed by everyone present, especially the people who knew I had no voice. The first few words spoken were whispered through the microphone. As I continued to open my mouth to speak my voice became stronger and stronger. I ended up speaking and praying over the people for almost three consecutive hours without any breaks. I think I even exceeded my designated time. The Lord Jesus manifested His loving presence powerfully. People were crying and experiencing His healing love throughout the talk. There was no doubt He was being glorified. I started praising and thanking Jesus, for truly NOTHING was impossible for Him. We were all witnesses. After my talk, the priest approached me with tears in his eyes and said: "*My daughter, before you started your talk, I was so worried because you had no voice. I didn't know what we were going to do! Then after you started talking and your voice miraculously came back, you kept on talking that I didn't know how to stop you.*" We both laughed and glorified God as we realized God's power manifesting through my weakness, or better said, my nothingness. Amazingly, as soon as my talk was over, I lost my voice again for the rest of the day. I hugged my friend Chayo after that and she repeated to me in amazement: "*Samia that was a miracle! That was a miracle! I knew you had no voice, but Jesus gave you a powerful voice, even though it didn't sound like you, and we all witnessed it!*"

This experience strengthened my faith even more and I realized that nothing will stop God from accomplishing His will. As long as I remained united to Him with a humble obedient heart and surrendered to His will, I would witness His glory wherever He sent me and regardless of my physical condition. I saw clearly that I was nothing without His grace! I was reminded of Jesus' words to St. Paul when He said: "*My grace is sufficient for you, for My power is made perfect in weakness.*" (2 Cor. 12:9). I also fully identified with St. Paul's response: "*I will all the more gladly boast of my weaknesses, that the power of Christ may rest upon me. For the sake of Christ, then, I am content with weaknesses, insults, hardships, persecutions, and calamities; for when I am weak, then I am strong.*" (2 Cor. 12:9–10)

Chapter 7

Trust in God's Providence

"And my God will fully satisfy every need of yours according to his riches in glory in Christ Jesus." — Phil. 4:19

My missions to Mexico were very powerful as I witnessed firsthand Jesus healing thousands of His children from deep childhood wounds and restoring them to who God created them to be. He reconciled many broken families and liberated many people from their addictions and vices. Many people, of all ages, experienced Jesus' love for the first time in their lives. Hundreds went to confession after many years and experienced God's infinite mercy. Even to this day, I still receive messages through Facebook and emails from people across Mexico whose lives were changed by God during one of my missions.

Upon my return from each mission, strange things would happen to me. It made me wonder if the devil was trying to retaliate against me. I never feared the devil as I knew Jesus defeated him on the cross and I always felt God's protection no matter what was going on around me. God always brought goodness out of every evil. God's children were no longer bound by the Father of lies and his deception.

One strange incident happened at the end of February 2010, two days after I had returned from Mexico. I had just left evening Mass with a friend and we were driving on the freeway to buy something. I wanted to catch up with my emails after my trip so I asked my friend to drive my car. We were driving about 70 miles per hour (MPH) when suddenly the Electronic Power Control (EPC) light came on, indicating a problem with the system that controlled the electronic throttle for the car. We suddenly lost power, and within seconds the car went down to 10 MPH on a busy freeway. My friend remained very calm and was able to carefully change lanes to pull over to a safe location. I was so grateful to God that I wasn't driving since without a doubt, I would have panicked. My car had to be towed to a mechanic, who told me it would cost $2,500 to repair it.

This was very upsetting since I didn't have an income like I did when I worked as a lawyer. I lived off of the donations that people gave me for my ministry, which barely paid for my monthly bills. I went to the Eucharistic Adoration Chapel to pray and complain to Jesus about my situation. I couldn't rely on my car as strange things were constantly happening to it. It was the only car I had to use for my travels throughout California for my different missions and it had to be reliable so I could feel safe while driving so often alone and late at night. After I finished venting, I heard Jesus tell me: "*Do not worry; you will have a new car soon.*" His words surprised me as I had no financial means to buy a new car. I couldn't even apply for a car loan. What was I supposed to say on the loan application when they asked me for my employer's name? Was I supposed to write "God?" What about my income level? Was I supposed to write "Divine Providence?" How was God going to give me a car? Was it going to appear suddenly in front of my house? I realized at that moment that I needed to stop trying to figure things out with my limited mind. I couldn't put God in a box with my human thinking. I just needed to be patient and trust Him.

Within a few weeks, I received a call from a married couple who wanted to meet with me on a Sunday at 8:00 AM in the morning. I was very surprised by their request as they lived several hours away from Sacramento. In order to meet with me at 8:00 AM, they would need to wake up before dawn to start their trip. I thought maybe they were having family problems and that was the reason they wanted to meet so early. I asked them to come at 9:00 AM to give me a chance to attend the 7:30 AM Mass.

When they arrived at my office, they looked very happy and positive. I thought to myself maybe they already resolved the problems they wanted to discuss with me. The husband proceeded to tell me the following story that led to their visit. One week earlier, they were attending a Catholic conference on Divine Mercy Sunday which was the Sunday that followed Easter. During the conference, they were listening to a speaker who shared his testimony. As part of his testimony, he shared how God had asked him to give his car to someone else in need. At that moment, the husband felt God asking him to buy me a car. Apparently, the couple had lent money years earlier to several family members and this loan had recently been repaid. The husband felt that God was asking him to use that money to buy me a car. However, the man wanted a clear confirmation from God to ensure he was hearing correctly. Therefore, he asked God in his heart that if He was asking him to do so, for God to give him another clear confirmation as he continued to listen to the speaker. After the speaker finished, as he was about to walk off the stage, he went back to the microphone and said the following: "*I want to repeat once again that God asked me to give my car away.*" At that moment, a sense of peace and joy consumed the heart of the husband. He shared with his wife what had just happened within his heart. His wife smiled and confirmed that she was also receiving the same message. They both felt God's joy and peace at once.

After they shared the story, they handed me an envelope saying: "*This is for you, from Jesus.*" When I opened the enveloped, I was astounded to see a check in my name for $20,000. I immediately placed the check back in the envelope and tried to give it back to them. I told them I couldn't accept it. They were hard-working people and had their own expenses and family obligations to take care of. They insisted and told me that I couldn't refuse Jesus' gift. They wanted to bring me the key to the car instead of a check but didn't know what kind of a vehicle I needed in light of all my missionary trips. That was the reason they wanted to see me so early in the morning. They wanted to accompany me to purchase the vehicle. At that moment, I was so overwhelmed with God's love and faithfulness to His promise to me to provide for *all* my daily needs. I wept tears of gratitude and embraced this wonderful couple, thanking them for their generosity and obedience to God. The couple was not related to me and they were not wealthy with extra money to give away. They had no ulterior motive to gift me with a car but they did it out of pure love and obedience to God. We went shopping afterwards and God guided us to a used Sports Utility Vehicle (SUV) that was in great condition and the perfect size to carry the boxes of my books and CDs that I carried with me to sell on my missions. The check covered the exact cost of the vehicle, including the taxes, registration and extended service warranty.

It became clear to me how when we are willing to open our hearts to God and are united to His will, He uses us in powerful ways for His glory. We become instruments of His love on earth to bless the lives of others and to fulfill His will. That's exactly what this couple did. Jesus moved their hearts to become His instruments to fulfill His promise to me when He had asked me to leave everything to serve Him. He promised to provide for all my daily needs. I needed a reliable car and He provided for me.

In fact, ever since I left my career, I have never lacked any necessities. God has *always* provided for me through the generosity of His faithful children. For example, in many instances, the donations I received from my speaking engagements or my individual sessions did not cover my monthly bills. I often spoke in places or prayed with people without receiving any donations. The Lord Jesus asked me to depend on Him. Amazingly, He always moved the heart of someone, who over the years was touched by my ministry, to send me unexpectedly a generous check to support me. This happened quite often over the years by many different people. The checks always came at the perfect moment and often were accompanied by a note stating something similar to this: "*I felt God was asking me to send you this donation to support your ministry.*" The donations I received were precisely what I needed that month to cover all my expenses. God has unlimited avenues and unusual ways of providing for our needs that extend beyond our natural limitations. All we need to do is trust Him. Jesus taught us in His sermon on the mountain: "*Therefore do not be anxious, saying, 'What shall we eat?' or 'What shall we drink?' or 'What shall we wear?' For the Gentiles seek all these things; and your heavenly Father knows that you need them all. But seek first his kingdom and his righteousness, and all these things shall be yours as well. Therefore do not be anxious about tomorrow, for tomorrow will be anxious for itself."* (Matthew 31–34)

Chapter 8

Physical Diseases and Disability

"We are afflicted in every way, but not crushed; perplexed, but not driven to despair; persecuted, but not forsaken; struck down, but not destroyed; always carrying in the body the death of Jesus, so that the life of Jesus may also be made visible in our bodies." — 2 Cor. 4:8–12

Growing up, I was a healthy person and I never had any significant health-related problems. However, upon returning from my mission in 2009, my physical condition began to decline and has continued to gradually worsen with each passing day. At first, I blamed the torn ligaments in my ankles for all my frequent falls, balance problems, and gait change. I was traveling to speak three or four times a week despite my physical pain, trying to ignore it and hoping that my ankles would get better with time.

One day, a friend noticed how unsteady my gait was, and she gave me some Epsom Salt. She suggested that I take a warm bath using the salt to help relax my body since I was doing so much traveling. I followed her advice and sat in my bathtub for a few minutes. Since the tub was uncomfortably small, I decided to get out as it was defeating the purpose of relaxation. When I tried to move my legs to get up, they were not responding. My brain was ordering my legs to move but they were paralyzed. I had a sinking feeling that there was something seriously wrong, much more severe than an ankle injury. When I was finally able to get out of the bathtub, I started to pray and asked Jesus to help me. Once I sat down and rested, I slowly recovered from the paralysis. I didn't mention anything to my parents at the time as I didn't want them to panic or worry about me.

The next day, I went to see my chiropractor for my weekly adjustment. I had been going for treatments for several weeks after someone had suggested it might help me recover my regular gait. Everyone who knew me noticed that I was walking in a strange way. When the chiropractor asked me how I was feeling, I recounted what transpired the night before in the bathtub. He was immediately concerned and suggested that my problem might be much more serious than just my ankle problem. He stated that I might have a neurological problem and advised me to be examined by a neurologist as soon as possible.

Usually it took weeks to obtain an appointment with a specialist, but I was able to obtain an appointment with a neurologist that same afternoon, which was a blessing from God! After examining me, the neurologist confirmed that it was clear from my reflex responses and my gait that I had a serious neurological problem, probably stemming from my neck. He told me that my symptoms were pointing to a very serious disease, but he didn't want to jump to conclusions without first obtaining MRI's of my neck and brain, doing a lumbar puncture (spinal tap) and many blood tests. Interestingly, my neck problems started when I was 11 years old when someone at school accidentally hit me in the neck with a basketball. I felt a discomfort in my neck and from that point on developed a habit of cracking it to release the tension and pain. I shared with the neurologist that since 2004, I had been feeling numbness and weakness in my left arm. At that time a doctor had diagnosed me with Degenerative Disc Disorder in my neck. I was referred to physical therapy, which didn't help, so I learned to live with the problem.

Within a few weeks, I met with my neurologist and a neurosurgeon regarding the results of the MRIs and the other tests. They confirmed I had multiple incurable diseases affecting my central nervous system (the brain, spinal cord and optic nerves). The neck MRI indicated I had cervical stenosis (five herniated discs) with myelopathy. Cervical stenosis is a slowly progressive condition that pinches the spinal cord in the neck. Cervical myelopathy refers to the compression of the cervical spinal cord as a result of spinal stenosis. People with cervical stenosis with myelopathy may have one or more of the following symptoms: heavy feeling in the legs, inability to walk at a brisk pace, deterioration in fine motor skills (such as handwriting or buttoning a shirt), intermittent shooting pains into the arms and legs (like an electrical shock), and arm pain. Unfortunately, I now suffer from all these symptoms.

I also had lesions on the spinal cord in my neck that extended from C2 to C6. The spinal fluid tests confirmed that I also had multiple sclerosis (MS). This is an unpredictable, often disabling disease of the central nervous system where the immune system attacks the protective sheath (myelin) that covers the nerves. Myelin damage disrupts communication between the brain and the rest of the body. Ultimately, the nerves themselves may deteriorate, a process that's currently irreversible and incurable.

MS is different for every person. Some may go through life with only minor problems, while others, like me, may become seriously disabled. Signs and symptoms vary widely, depending on the amount of damage and which nerves are affected. MS signs and symptoms include: numbness or weakness in one or both legs or arms, partial or complete loss of vision, usually in one eye at a time, tingling or pain in parts of the body, electric shock sensations that occur with certain neck movements, especially bending the neck forward, tremor, spasm, stiffness, lack of coordination or unsteady gait, extreme fatigue, sensitivity to hot or cold weather, and problems with bowel and bladder functions. As of the present moment, I suffer daily from all the symptoms mentioned with the exception of the vision problems, which I will discuss in Chapter 10.

The neurologist explained to me the four different types of MS. He told me I had the worst type, primary progressive MS, which affected about 10% of the MS patients. It is characterized by steady continuous worsening of neurologic functioning, without any distinct relapses (attacks) or periods of remission. Currently, there are no medications for this type of MS. The majority of MS patients (about 85%) have the relapse-remitting type, which has many approved medications to control the attacks and inflammation. However, with primary progressive MS, none of these medications have been beneficial, as this type of MS is characterized by nerve degeneration rather than inflammation. The neurologist told me there was nothing they could give me or do for me as I had permanent extensive nerve damage already. My two diseases displayed very similar symptoms, so my case was quite complicated and difficult.

I also met with the neurosurgeon to discuss the cervical stenosis. He informed me that my case was very bad, especially in light of the distinct diseases I had. He suggested a surgery involving decompression which might not improve the symptoms, especially since I still had MS. Typically, the main goal of cervical spinal stenosis surgery was to arrest the progressive nature of the condition and stabilize the neurological condition. He told me that there was always a risk that I could be left paralyzed by the surgery. He also didn't think "I had much time left" considering all the nerve damage and how it would eventually affect the signals to my organs and the rest of my body. I told him I needed to pray about the surgery in order to discern God's will. He asked me not to take too long to consider the surgery as it might be too late within a few months.

I walked out of the neurosurgeon's office very agitated and robbed of my inner peace. I had to hold on to the hospital walls to sustain myself, and I felt that I was given a death sentence and my whole world seemed to be collapsing. I repeated continuously in my heart "*Jesus, I trust in You*" which gave me strength to reach my car. As soon as I sat in my car, I closed my eyes and tried to focus only on Jesus and not on my diagnosis or the words of the neurosurgeon. Jesus reminded me of His words to me in 2005 when I was in prayer at the Adoration Chapel: "*No matter how many emergency sirens are going off around you, whether in your own personal life, or in the physical world around you, just keep your eyes fixed on Me! Do NOT*

50

fear anything. Focus your eyes on Me always. I will get you through all the situations and provide you with all the protection you need."

The emergency sirens were sounding in my personal life like never before, and I needed to remain focused on Jesus. I drove straight to the Eucharistic Adoration Chapel to be with my Lord Jesus and pray about my medical situation. As soon as I arrived inside, I prostrated myself before Jesus in the Blessed Sacrament and surrendered my life to Him again in its entirety, including my health. I said: "*My Lord Jesus, You gave me life and I re-surrender it to You. If it is time for me to depart from this world, let Your will be done in my life. Just give me a confirmation so that I can cancel all the speaking engagements that I have in conferences and retreats in the upcoming weeks and months to give the organizers sufficient time to find a replacement. Please let me know if I should have the surgery. I don't have inner peace about it.*"

Jesus spoke to my heart the following words: "*Do not be afraid. Nothing can happen to you in your life without My permission. Your illness is for My glory. Do not be afraid. I will heal you. Remain always united to Me.*" His words flooded my soul with peace. I knew I was in His hands and there was a purpose for my illness and suffering. These terrible diseases were not coming from Him, but He was allowing them in my life for a purpose, and I needed to trust Him and proceed with my agenda as planned. Jesus also said He would heal me, but didn't specify the timeframe or the method. In my mind, I knew there were two types of healing: the temporary one on earth and the permanent and ultimate one when we depart to eternal life. I assumed Jesus was referring to an earthly healing for me.

I continued to pray with people in my office and also to travel across the United States and Mexico for an additional year. With each passing day, I became more disabled and my pain rose to more excruciating levels of physical suffering. The hardest part was adjusting every day to my declining physical condition. After falling frequently, often at airports and at conferences, I was forced to use a cane to support myself. I had no balance and was becoming weaker each day. The cane didn't give me enough stability, so in a very short time I was compelled to use a walker. At first, it was difficult for me to be seen publicly using a walker, but I quickly realized it was much more humiliating to fall in public places if I didn't use the walker. There was no doubt in my mind that God was continuing to strip me from my ego.

My health and independence were things I believed were a given in my life. The diseases were progressing in my body so rapidly; however, my mind couldn't process or adjust fast enough. I constantly needed to make adjustments to my everyday life, like giving myself extra time to go anywhere. Also, I would get tired very soon even with the assistance of my walker, and I started avoiding going outside in the heat as it aggravated my symptoms. I could no longer wear clothes with buttons because my loss of fine motor skills in both hands meant that I couldn't button my clothes anymore. When I was in airports, taking a few steps, even with my walker, became exhausting to me and I started asking for wheelchair assistance each time I traveled. I was rapidly losing muscle in my body, especially in my legs and my core. The simple task of picking things up from the floor became harder each day. Excruciating pain and stiffness ravaged every part of my body.

I read many books on multiple sclerosis and natural treatments and tried changing my diet, taking natural herbal supplements, but to no avail. It seemed that many natural treatments helped the relapse-remittance type of MS, but the type I had seemed to be irreversible, as my condition continued to gradually worsen.

One day after attending noon Mass, a lady I had seen before asked me if I would give her a ride back to her work from church—at the time, I was still able to drive despite my condition. I was happy to do this, and during the drive, she asked me about my medical condition since she noted that I was having problems walking. I explained to her about my health issues, she immediately asked me if I had heard of a physician named Dr. Issam Nemeh who had been recently featured on the television program "Dr. Oz." She explained that he was a medical doctor who also had the gift of healing and many patients with incurable diseases were miraculously healed after he prayed for them. At first I was very skeptical and asked her if this was New Age healing, as I had many concerns with that. She responded he was a Catholic doctor who invoked the Holy Spirit and prayed in the name of Jesus. She took my email address and said she would email me information as soon as she got to her work.

When I arrived at my office, I had an email awaiting me with some YouTube videos on Dr. Nemeh. As I listened to him, I knew in my heart he was authentic. He seemed humble and filled with God's love. In one of his interviews he was asked about his gift of healing, and his response impressed me: "*I do not recognize any gift at all. Even though it is written and is biblically sound, I think it needs to be redefined. It's not about a gift, it is about true belonging. Belonging to the Body of Christ is such a real thing. It is not a figurative image. When we belong, we offer ourselves automatically to that Body, and the Head of that Body will communicate Himself to us as part of Him. And that communication actually takes place through the Holy Spirit. We are praying for the manifestation of God in our lives. The healing that happens is the sign of the presence of God amongst us.*"

After I finished my research on Dr. Nemeh, I called his medical office in Cleveland, Ohio to see if I could make an urgent appointment with him. I had a month-long mission trip to Mexico approaching and I wondered if God was going to use him to heal me before my trip as my physical condition was worsening. I left a message with my contact information, and to my surprise, Dr. Nemeh's wife, Kathy, returned my call later that evening. She informed me that Dr. Nemeh was booked for at least a year and invited me to attend one of the healing services he held across the country to meet people's demand. I responded that I had to leave for Mexico within 10 days and I was willing to fly to their next healing service in Chicago. Kathy was very loving and kind and gave me her personal number to contact her once I arrived. She invited me to stay for all the healing services throughout the weekend. When I was in prayer before my trip, the Lord Jesus confirmed to me that it was part of His plan for me to meet Dr. Nemeh, since I would be learning important spiritual lessons from him that would help me reach the next spiritual level.

Indeed, my weekend in Chicago was filled with many blessings and lessons. Before each healing service, Dr. Nemeh gave an enlightening talk followed by questions and answers about the Holy Trinity, the fall of Satan and one-third of the angels, why God permits suffering, and the importance of our state of mind. I had no doubt that our Lord Jesus worked powerfully through Dr. Nemeh's full surrender to Him. I witnessed the love of Christ radiating through him as he answered people's questions after his talk and then patiently prayed all weekend long over hundreds of people individually. When he prayed over me, he immediately placed his hand on my neck and invoked the Holy Spirit praying for my healing even though he had no prior knowledge of my medical diagnosis. I felt an incredible feeling of peace and love consume my body. I wasn't fully healed, but I felt stronger. It's important to mention that not everyone receives a physical healing during the services but many people experience some kind of a healing, whether it is physical, emotional or spiritual.

Kathy Nemeh arranged for me to meet and talk with Dr. Nemeh privately after his healing services. He reviewed my MRI results, and upon my return from my mission to Mexico, he arranged for me to meet him at his medical clinic for treatment despite the long waiting list. The Lord Jesus never told me that Dr. Nemeh was going to heal me—even though that was what I had hoped—but I felt significantly better and stronger after each treatment. However, Jesus said that Dr. Nemeh would teach me spiritual lessons that would enable me to reach the next spiritual level. The experience crystallized for me many valuable lessons, of which the following have been important in helping me grow spiritually in spite of my physical condition and suffering:

- **The importance of totally surrendering our lives to God:** We must surrender in the smallest details of our lives, not just large details, offering everything to Christ, including illness and death. Everything happens for a blessed reason when we surrender ourselves to Jesus. If Jesus is allowing something in our lives, then it's a blessing. Once we have that discipline of mind, we will always live in peace and will automatically see God's hand in everything.

- **Steadiness and peace:** No matter what happens, it's important to be still and fill ourselves with God's love daily through all the circumstances of life. Peace is not about being happy or not suffering. It's the result of faith in God. *"Be still, and know that I am God!"* (Psalm 46:10)

- **When healing doesn't occur:** Sometimes miracles take a little bit longer because there is something else we have to learn. We must listen in silence, pay attention and learn. We have to look at the illness as a blessing, an experience that holds a great spiritual lesson. As St. Paul said: *"We know that in everything God works for good with those who love him, who are called according to his purpose."* (Rom. 8:28)

- **The importance of our state of mind:** This is the way we think, the way we actually look at the world and everyone around us, and how we interact with them. When we manifest the right type of thinking with everyone around us—loving and caring about everyone and everything around us—we align ourselves with the mind of God who is love. Our human mind is such a powerful gift from God the Father, the all-knowing and eternal mind. We reach a perfect state of mind when we surrender ourselves and our experiences totally to the will of God, recognizing His will in everything. If our mind is connected to the perfect love of God, then there is no power that can violate us physically or spiritually.

- **The greatest healing:** The greatest healing isn't the healing of our body but the healing of our mind.

- **Why God allows Suffering:** Suffering has inestimable redemptive worth and nothing equals it in heaven or on earth. When we join our sufferings to Christ's infinite merits, we intimately participate in God's plan of salvation. God works through us to obtain spiritual merits for the conversion of our family members and others in the Body of Christ who are living away from Him. As St. Paul expressed: "*Now I rejoice in my sufferings for your sake, and in my flesh I complete what is lacking in Christ's afflictions for the sake of his body, that is, the church.*" (Col. 1:24)

Dr. Nemeh confirmed to me that Jesus would heal me, but first I had to learn some spiritual lessons. Clearly, I needed to apply all that I was learning from Dr. Nemeh to my situation by surrendering all the details of my life to God, by being still in God's peace and love, and by always maintaining a loving state of mind. I also needed to remain open to all additional lessons to be learned from the experience of my diseases and disability.

Chapter 9

Overcoming Adversity

"Be still, and know that I am God!" — Psalm 46:10

My life became more difficult with each passing day but I took refuge in Jesus. I knew He was always with me and would never abandon me, although on many days, my pain seemed unbearable. I refused to take any prescription painkillers since I knew they were a temporary solution. I didn't want to become addicted to them and I strongly disliked the side effects. I once took a prescription painkiller and felt very disconnected spiritually, as if I had no soul. It's crucial for my prayer life and my ministry for me to remain lucid and connected to my heart where I communicate with my Lord Jesus. With time, I believed I would build my tolerance for pain.

At the end of December 2011, I hit rock bottom and felt buried under the weight of my cross instead of carrying it. I experienced an overwhelming sadness in my heart as I realized how lonely my journey had become. Even though I was surrounded by people, nobody seemed to understand how I was feeling or what I was enduring each day. Only Jesus fully comprehended me. I felt extremely exhausted, with nothing more to give, and it became very difficult for me to focus on the lessons that I needed to learn. I made the grave mistake of falling into a "victim mentality." My focus became my declining physical condition and the difficulties I was facing each day, turning away from Jesus and making me susceptible to the attacks of the enemy.

One evening, I went to the Eucharistic Adoration Chapel and tearfully opened my heart to Jesus about my feelings. I said: "*My Lord Jesus, I thank You for the life You have gifted me. Thank You for all the things I have learned so far. I have lived a fulfilled life with many invaluable experiences, but now I feel completely wiped out and buried beneath my cross. The suffering has been more difficult than I could have ever imagined. As You know already, I don't have any children or a husband who rely on me or need me. If my time has come to leave to my eternal home, I am ready to go. I have done everything You have asked me to do.*"

The Lord Jesus responded: "*Your time has not come yet and You still have a lot of work to do on earth.*" In my mind's eye, I had a vision of a multitude of people standing in front of me, too numerous to count, and I couldn't see their faces or discern their nationality. Jesus then added: "*These children of Mine will soon come before Me but they are not spiritually ready. Are you willing to suffer more for them?*" I responded without any hesitation with a strong "yes" and asked Him to give me extra graces to enable me to carry my heavy cross with joy and love. Instantly, a great sense of peace flooded my soul, melting away all the sadness I had been feeling and renewing my strength and determination. In my heart, I sensed that the extra suffering was going to be for a temporary period.

Amazingly, even though my condition worsened significantly, my attitude about this decline became radically different. The vision that Jesus showed me gave me a greater understanding of the value of my suffering. Even though I knew intellectually that God used the suffering we offered Him for a greater purpose, the vision helped me see it and understand it with my heart. I finally understood St. Paul's words: "*Now I rejoice in my sufferings for your sake, and in my flesh I complete what is lacking in Christ's afflictions for the sake of his body, that is, the church*" (Col. 1:24). When we offer our suffering—the one thing most disagreeable to our human nature—back to God, it becomes a gift of inestimable value, drawing down from heaven more graces than any other action we can possibly make. I joked once with a friend about one of my diseases saying that I had MS and the acronym in a spiritual sense stood for: More Suffering = More Souls.

When we lovingly surrender everything in our lives to God, our suffering, even in the smallest of tasks, has a great value. After attending Sunday Mass on a very hot summer day in 2012, I was anxious to get home since the heat worsened my symptoms significantly. I also urgently needed to use the restroom and had bladder control problems. At that time, I was much weaker but still able to walk with a walker. When I reached for my key to unlock the door, I dropped it on the ground due to the loss of fine motor skills in my hands, which is one of the many symptoms of MS. I tried to reach down to the ground to pick up my keys but my legs were too weak to allow me that simple movement. I looked around to see if any of my neighbors were outside to assist me but the street was empty. The only way I could reach my keys was for me to drop my body to the ground and pick them up. I did just that. However, I had another problem; I didn't have enough strength in my legs to get myself back up. I wanted to use my walker to help me get up, but on that day, I had a lighter walker because I could load it in the car unassisted. However, this lighter walker was not strong enough to support my weight. I tried to extend my upper body to unlock the door, and after struggling for 10 minutes, I finally succeeded in opening it. I crawled to get my body inside the house to get away from the heat that was draining the little strength I had left.

Inside the house, I tried several times to hold on to the walls in order to push myself up. I came close to standing up several times but would fall back again, banging my arms and body against the walls and ground. With each passing second, I felt the pressure of my merciless bladder which was adding more pressure and urgency to the situation. Finally, I crawled towards a chair that had arms I could hold on to and after several attempts, I was able to push myself up and sit. Once I recovered some strength, I was able to stand up and use my walker to reach the restroom but it was too late. I closed my eyes and turned to my heart to ask Jesus what lesson was behind this unexpected ordeal. I knew that He was going to teach me something important because He always sent me help before whenever I needed it. Picking up a key from the ground was a simple act even a one-year old child could perform. It usually would take a healthy person less than 10 seconds to pick up a key and go inside a house, but in my situation, it took almost an hour and I had bruises all over my arms and body from all the bumping against the walls and ground. Jesus said: *"Only when you join Me in heaven will you get to see how many souls were saved today through the merits of your suffering and surrender to My will."* This lesson was very important to me because I realized the value of suffering through everything we endure in life. No matter how small or insignificant it might seem to us, when we surrender to the will of God, other souls benefit from our sacrifices. Isn't this the same lesson Jesus taught us on the cross centuries ago, yet we manage to pay little attention to it in our daily lives? This spiritual awareness encouraged me to maintain peace in my heart under all conditions. No matter how unbearable my suffering would become later, I understood that all suffering offered up to God would never be wasted.

In April of 2012, Lorena, the manager of *Radio Santísimo Sacramento* (Radio of the Most Holy Sacrament), the Spanish radio station owned by the Catholic Diocese of Sacramento, asked me to host my own radio program on inner healing. It was called *Sanación del Alma* (Healing of the Soul), and it aired on Friday mornings. I gladly accepted the offer, not knowing that four months later, due to the rapid decline in my health, my radio program would become my only form of public ministry. I still maintained my presence on social media, particularly Facebook, which I used to inspire others via my daily spiritual posts. I also assisted many people who sent me messages daily asking for prayers or assistance with their personal problems.

On my program which as of this writing is on the air every Friday and Tuesday morning, I openly discuss all topics related to inner healing such as: divorce, abandonment, rejection, child abuse (physical, emotional, sexual), incest, alcoholism, abortion, addictions, bullying and many other topics. I take listener's calls live on the air and pray with them for their healing or their prayer petitions. The program rapidly became very popular as the word spread, and eventually I had listeners tune in via the internet from all across the United States, Mexico, Central and South American countries and even Spain. I frequently receive messages via Facebook from my listeners, sharing how much they are learning from my program and how the Lord Jesus has healed them through a prayer I said over a caller who suffered from a wound similar to theirs. Jesus was multiplying the healings and blessings in ways I could have never anticipated.

It never ceases to amaze me how the Lord Jesus plans every detail of my life. When I started my radio program, I could never have foreseen that my health was going to decline so rapidly to the extent of preventing me from traveling. However, Jesus is always many steps ahead of me and provides me with a radio program where I am able to minister to thousands of people all over the world despite my severe disability and physical limitations.

As my physical condition worsened, it became extremely painful for me to get to the radio station where there was a small flight of stairs to climb in order to get to the studio. The radio station is located in one of the old buildings owned by the Sanctuary of our Lady of Guadalupe in Sacramento. I attend morning Mass at the sanctuary immediately preceding my radio program. With each passing week, as my disability worsened and my physical pain dramatically increased, people who worked at the radio station or others who were leaving Mass assisted me, as my suffering was visible. As I climbed each step, I felt like someone was violently ripping each muscle out of my lower body, and by the time I would get to the final step, I would often be in tears as the pain was beyond human words. I knew it was Jesus' grace that was sustaining me, and the only thought that carried me through the torturous experience was Jesus' thirst for souls.

After my program was on the air for a year, I prayed to our Lord Jesus to help me with my situation. Even though I wished to continue serving Him through the radio program, climbing the stairs was becoming an impossible task for me and I contemplated cancelling my weekly program. When I went to the radio station one Friday, I asked Jesus to reveal to me His will because after my program, I intended to speak with Lorena about my situation and the possibility of cancelling my program. Just before the show started, Lorena joyfully told me that my show had the highest number of listeners and that one hour a week was insufficient to meet the needs of all the callers. She proposed that I host my program on Tuesdays in addition to Fridays. I explained to her my difficulty with the stairs, and she suggested that we could ask for donations from the listeners during my program for the purchase of an electric stair lift. Lorena made the announcement at the beginning of my program, and amazingly, by the end of the program, listeners had called in to contribute to the cost of the lift. Some even came to the station to make their donations before my program was over. Within a week, enough donations were made to buy the stair lift.

I praised God for the love and generosity of the radio listeners and also smiled at God's sense of humor. That day I went to the station with the intention of cancelling my program on Fridays and instead I returned home with an additional day added for my show. Clearly, it wasn't God's will for me to cancel but rather to work through my surrender in a much greater capacity. Using my physical limitations and suffering to inspire many people and touch their hearts. During my program, I started sharing the details of my physical condition and how Jesus' graces made it possible for me to continue going to the radio to help others. The process of getting ready in the mornings to go to Mass and my radio show was extremely painful and often seemed impossible. Every movement in my body was very painful and took much effort. I am convinced that if it wasn't for my union with Jesus and His graces, I would have been going to the emergency room instead of the radio station. Even my father who assisted me on these early mornings and witnessed my suffering and the effort it took for me to get ready told me, "*I admire your faith and perseverance, and I have no doubt in my mind that God's graces are supernaturally sustaining you.*"

Nothing was going to stand in the way of fulfilling God's will. Even when I couldn't drive anymore, my friend Eliana who works for the radio, started picking me up and driving me home after my program. Several people who work or volunteer at the station help each time in transferring me into the chair lift and back into my wheelchair. Through my disability, I experienced the love of many people who volunteered to assist me at the radio and even offered to help me with my personal chores. Many radio listeners and others who see me, tell me they are inspired by my witness of how joyfully and lovingly I carry my cross despite my suffering, and when they are being tested, they think of me and obtain strength from my testimony. In fact, as time passed, I used my own experiences to give the radio listeners spiritual tools to help them deal with their life's storms and difficulties, and strengthen them spiritually to overcome their adversities.

One indispensable tool is prayer, which is as important to our soul as the oxygen is to our bodies! God pours out His graces and understanding into our soul through prayer and arms us against the enemy's attacks. Without prayer, our soul has no strength! When we have a deep spiritual life through prayer and communion with God, we will have a clearer understanding of the purpose of the storms in our lives, especially our suffering. As St. Pope John Paul II once said: *"Prayer joined to sacrifice constitutes the most powerful force in human history."* The Rosary, for instance, is a very powerful prayer to fight evil, especially addictions, division and family problems. This is a Catholic prayer that meditates on the life and various events of Jesus' life, taken directly from the New Testament of the Bible. They are called the Mysteries of the Rosary and are divided into four main parts. The Joyful Mysteries contemplate the first twelve years of Jesus' life, the Luminous Mysteries contemplate His three years of ministry as He fulfilled His mission on earth, the Sorrowful Mysteries contemplate His agony, passion, crucifixion and death, and finally, the Glorious Mysteries contemplate His resurrection and ascension into heaven. The Rosary is prayed on "rosary beads," and is a meditation on Jesus' life. It is a powerful tool against the devil who cannot tolerate this prayer. Praying the Rosary has been essential on my spiritual journey and has often led to miraculous results, one of which I will discuss in the following chapter.

Other essential spiritual tools for me have been the Sacraments of the Holy Eucharist and Confession (Penance). A "Sacrament" is a sign of grace, instituted by Jesus and entrusted to the Church, by which divine life is dispensed to us. Since 2002, I made a commitment to attend daily Mass to receive Jesus in the Eucharist. The Eucharist is the spiritual food that nourishes my eternal soul. Just like I eat daily to nourish my body, maintain my strength and survive physically, I need to receive the Eucharist frequently, daily if possible, to nourish and strengthen my soul. As Jesus told us through His apostle John: "*Truly, truly, I say to you, unless you eat the flesh of the Son of man and drink his blood, you have no life in you; he who eats my flesh and drinks my blood has eternal life, and I will raise him up at the last day. For my flesh is food indeed, and my blood is drink indeed. He who eats my flesh and drinks my blood abides in me, and I in him. As the living Father sent me, and I live because of the Father, so he who eats me will live because of me. This is the bread which came down from heaven, not such as the fathers ate and died; he who eats this bread will live forever.*" (John 6:53—58).

The Sacrament of Confession has been indispensable to me as well. It is a cleansing and healing spiritual gift from Jesus, where we reconcile with Him and experience His unlimited mercy. Catholics believe that the Lord Jesus, through a priest, hears our sins and pardons us. Even though the priest is also a sinner and just a human being, the Lord uses him as an instrument to channel His love and mercy. It is actually a very humbling experience for me to confess my sins before another human being, regardless of how sinful or holy the other person is. Pride has been my enemy over the years, so I welcome all experiences that assist me in ridding myself of it. Jesus said to His apostles: "*Receive the Holy Spirit. If you forgive the sins of any, they are forgiven; if you retain the sins of any, they are retained.*" (John 6:22—23). I confess my sins frequently, at least monthly. Just like I shower regularly to keep my physical body clean and healthy to avoid illness, I also try to keep my eternal soul clean and healthy to hear the voice of God clearly within my heart and to avoid spiritual sickness.

I have no doubt that these spiritual tools have given me divine graces to defy natural laws by strengthening and purifying my soul and by helping me cross over from the natural to the supernatural. The more I die to myself, the greater is Jesus' manifestation through my surrender. One day, a radio listener called my show to share her testimony. She was suffering for a long time from deep bleeding (hemorrhage) and sharp pain. She saw me at one of the radio station public events and approached me to ask me to pray for her. As I hugged her, she felt something happen inside her body and her pain suddenly disappeared. When she arrived at her home, she realized that her bleeding had fully stopped and never returned. I praised and glorified our Lord Jesus for healing her through our embrace. Once again, in my nothingness, He was being glorified. I have received many other testimonies of healing, whether physical or emotional. Jesus is as alive today as He was when lived on earth over 2000 years ago. I don't know how long my radio program will continue but one thing I'm certain of is that I witness Jesus' presence and glory in my life with each breath and movement of my body. I wonder often if this is how St. Paul was feeling when he said: "*I have been crucified with Christ; it is no longer I who live, but Christ who lives in me; and the life I now live in the flesh I live by faith in the Son of God, who loved me and gave himself for me.*" (Gal. 2:20)

Each day is a living miracle to me and I have never felt such inner peace, joy and unconditional love for others as I do today. Truly, *nothing* separates me from the love of Christ!

Chapter 10

Miraculous Healing from Blindness

"For nothing will be impossible with God." —Luke 1:37

In April 2013, I was contacted by my neurologist regarding my vision. He wanted to schedule additional exams for my optic nerves since he suspected I might have a more severe illness that mimics MS called neuromyelitis optica (NMO). NMO is a rare autoimmune disorder in which immune system cells and antibodies mistakenly attack and destroy myelin cells in the optic nerves and the spinal cord. The damage to the optic nerves results in swelling and inflammation that cause pain and loss of vision; the damage to the spinal cord causes weakness or paralysis in the legs or arms, loss of sensation, and problems with bladder and bowel function.

The neurologist noted that my physical condition was declining very rapidly and suspected I might have been misdiagnosed. Even though I told him that I had never experienced any vision problems before, he urged me to have an EEG test that detects electrical activity in my brain. The EEG test results were very abnormal, indicating that the disease that was damaging my spinal cord was also damaging the path from the eyes to the brain. He told me I could go blind in one or both eyes at any moment and suggested that I should start a chemotherapy treatment of IV infusions as soon as possible. These treatments would suppress my immune system in an effort to stop the rapid decline in my health. Chemotherapy wouldn't heal me or make me feel better; it would only suppress my immune system so that my antibodies would stop attacking the spinal and optic nerves causing more paralysis or blindness. It was recommended that I receive two doses about two weeks apart at the hospital and then repeat the process every six months, for as long as I lived.

Something about the news that the neurologist shared with me didn't feel right, especially the chemotherapy treatments to suppress my immune system *for life*. This course of treatment would make me more susceptible to bacterial or viral infections, developing cancer, or having a flu that turns into a deadly pneumonia. I never had unusual vision problems and I have also tested negative to the NMO antibody. The neurologist explained that 30% of the people test negative but still have the disease, and even though I never experienced vision problems, the damage was severe and I could lose my vision at any moment. The neurologist told me he had already discussed my case with the Neurology Department doctors at the hospital, and they all agreed that my situation was very complicated and suggested I get a second opinion, which was what I did. The second neurologist had an excellent bedside manner and validated my concerns about the chemotherapy treatment. He believed it was too harsh and had many side effects. He also couldn't be certain I had NMO instead of MS, as my case was very complicated and he didn't want me to start chemotherapy treatments if I didn't have NMO.

As I prayed about my situation, I decided on the option that gave me inner peace, which was to decline chemotherapy. Inner peace is the fruit of doing God's will even in the midst of great trials and tribulations. I just didn't want to open myself up to more diseases than the ones I already had. I decided not to tell my parents or siblings the news. I was afraid they would push me to undergo chemotherapy out of their love for me and a desire to prolong my life. For me, I preferred to have a "better" quality of life than a longer one potentially ravaged by even more diseases.

Three months later, toward the end of July 2013, I started having blurry vision in my right eye and it slowly worsened each day. Initially I thought it was normal since I was in my early forties and assumed I was starting to develop farsightedness and needed reading glasses. On August 22, 2014, I had an appointment with the ophthalmologist to examine my eyes. When the doctor initially checked the vision in my right eye by asking me to read the chart, I couldn't read any of the letters. Concerned, he switched to the chart that had only the large size letter "E" and asked me to read it. Frankly, I couldn't even tell that he switched the chart as I couldn't see or read anything with that eye, as if it had a blank white sheet covering it. The doctor knew right away I had more serious issues with my eye. He read my medical chart and suggested that my vision problem was due to damage in my optic nerves. He dilated my pupils to do a more detailed exam and the results were discouraging. He said action should be taken as soon as possible, and telephoned an ophthalmologist who specialized in issues related to optic nerves. The specialist agreed to examine my eyes right away. I had permanent damage to my nerves and I was legally blind in my right eye with 20/400 vision. The specialist was concerned that the same thing could happen to my left eye, so he scheduled me for another visual field exam in six weeks. The specialist believed my optic nerve damage was permanent and sent me home without a prescription for steroid medication. Steroids work by weakening the immune system and reducing inflammation around the site of nerve damage. Since my immune system was already compromised, this course of treatment would be counterproductive.

I went home after my appointment feeling crushed. Being mostly paralyzed was already extremely difficult, but adding blindness to that situation didn't feel right to me. I closed my eyes and contemplated the "NMO" acronym of the new diagnosis that I was given and asked the Holy Spirit to reveal to me what these three letters in the acronym stood for spiritually. Immediately these three words came clearly into my heart: "*No More Oppression.*" I knew what the word oppression meant but I was prompted to look up its meaning in the dictionary. It said: "unjust or cruel exercise of authority or power; something that oppresses especially in being an unjust or excessive exercise of power." Then I looked at the synonym of the word and the first word listed was "blue devils." I couldn't believe my eyes especially seeing the word "devil." I felt there was something demonic about the diagnosis ever since the neurologist told me in April that he suspected I had NMO instead of MS and I could go blind at any moment. Reading the definition of the word "oppression" confirmed to me on a spiritual level that the devil was trying to oppress me more by exercising unjust and excessive power so that I would go fully blind in addition to all my other challenges.

I sat in my room before the image of our Blessed Mother Mary. She is my beloved spiritual mother who took me to her Son Jesus in a profound way in Medjugorje, which transformed my life. I told her that I couldn't believe I was getting such bad news on her feast day on August 22, the day Roman Catholics celebrate the Queenship of the Blessed Virgin Mary. I knew this blindness was not part of the will of God and I felt I had to fight back. As I prayed more, the Holy Spirit reminded me of what the Blessed Virgin Mary said in her apparitions in Medjugorje: "*My children, through prayer and fasting one can stop wars and can suspend the laws of nature.*"

I understood right away that our Blessed Mother Mary was giving me the spiritual tools to fight back. If prayer and fasting could stop wars and suspend the laws of nature, then prayer and fasting would restore my vision! The next day, I started a novena (nine days) of prayer and fasting and I fasted strictly on bread and water, each day offering my illness and suffering to God as a prayer. I also prayed and meditated every day on the 20 mysteries of the Rosary. I knew that the devil hated this powerful prayer since it was like a spiritual weapon that would kill the demons roaming around us. God gave me the graces I needed to persevere in fasting despite my health condition, and I was determined to resist all the "temptations" of my mom's delicious homemade food that surrounded me daily. On the fifth day of my novena, there was a significant improvement in my vision and by the ninth day, I had approximately 80% of my vision back. A few days later, my vision was fully restored and seemed clearer than ever. I began praising and glorifying God! I knew without a doubt that my Blessed Mother Mary interceded for me before her Son, Jesus, who healed my optic nerves and fully restored my vision. During the novena, my neurologist contacted me and informed me that he was being transferred to another location in a neighboring city. He told me that if his new location was inconvenient for me, he could refer me to the neurologist who gave me the second opinion. I was elated and praised God, as I knew this was another by-product of my novena. I felt more of a connection with the second neurologist and had wished in my heart that he was my primary neurologist. Clearly, Jesus responded to the whispers of my heart and granted that wish.

Six weeks later, I went back for another visual field exam to assess the damage in my eyes, especially my optic nerves, and visual pathways to the brain. After the specialist reviewed my results, he said there was remarkable improvement in my right eye and even my other eye had improved! Eight months later he gave me another thorough exam, and he and his assisting nurse were completely amazed. Both eyes and optic nerves were completely healthy, and my vision was a perfect 20/20—better than what it was before my illness! They had no explanation of how my optic nerves and my vision were restored. I told them that Jesus had healed me after I prayed and fasted for nine days, and my restored sight was a proof of His miraculous healing. The specialist agreed with me that the healing was miraculous since there was no other scientific explanation and then he asked me to pray for his health before I left his office.

Soon thereafter, I had an appointment with my second neurologist to discuss my case. He was elated that my vision and optic nerves were fully restored and agreed that there was no medical explanation for my healing. As far as the rest of my body, he was not fully convinced that my new diagnosis was accurate. Even though I was not entitled to another second opinion, he referred me to an expert neurologist in San Francisco, who specialized in MS and NMO cases. This neurologist thoroughly reviewed my medical file, asking me many questions and examining me. Her conclusion was that I had primary progressive MS and not NMO, since NMO was not a progressive disease but a relapse one, marked by "attacks" and then periods of remission. I was grateful to God that I trusted my heart in April and declined chemotherapy which would have caused me more damage without stopping the progression of my MS. I was very grateful to my Lord Jesus for His unceasing love and protection and for healing and restoring my vision to perfection. With every passing day, I am more in love with Him!

I join King David in praising God when he glorified Him saying: "*I will extol you, my God and King, and bless your name forever and ever. Every day I will bless you, and praise your name forever and ever. Great is the Lord, and greatly to be praised; his greatness is unsearchable.*" (Psalm 145:1–3)

Chapter 11

The Paradox of the Cross

"The message of the cross is foolishness to those who are perishing, but to us who are being saved it is the power of God." — 1 Cor. 1:18

God **permits** suffering as a means for our purification and sanctification. It gives us an entirely different awareness of life and its seriousness. The reason we exist on earth isn't only to have families and children, careers, houses, power and wealth, or become famous. **Rather, we are on earth to learn to know and love God and love other humans through all of life's experiences.** God, at the end of our lives, won't ask us about our bank accounts, professions or earthly achievements. He will ask us one question. *How much did you love?* That's why there is suffering. For only the one who knows how to suffer knows how to love. To look upon the cross is not only to look upon suffering, but to look upon unconditional perfect love, which resulted in our salvation.

Often, whenever my cross in life seems too heavy, I sit before a crucifix and contemplate Jesus' agony in the garden, His passion, crucifixion, and death. He demonstrated by His example and surrender, what perfect and unconditional love looks like. Jesus never asked us to do anything that He didn't do Himself on earth. When I contemplate all the torture and suffering that Jesus, the sinless One, endured for our sins out of pure love for us, I am strengthened to carry my own cross with love. While we should not seek suffering in itself, it can nonetheless be of great value in perfecting our love, purifying all that is not love, and building up the Body of Christ.

Through my suffering, especially during my illness, I have grown spiritually and emotionally in profound ways more than in any other period in my life. I cannot view life with earthly eyes anymore but only through a spiritual lens. There is a spiritual lesson to be learned from everything we experience on earth, so it's always important to ask ourselves the question: "*What am I supposed to learn from this situation?*" God may be calling us to turn our lives to Him, to repent, or to grow in grace or in one of the virtues, (e.g. faith hope or love), or to forgive others or even ourselves, or to break out of a sinful habit or situation that is destroying our soul. When we only focus on the problem, we often waste many opportunities to grow spiritually. I would like to share some of the spiritual lessons I have learned, in addition to the ones I stated in Chapter 8, and the fruits that suffering has borne in my life.

- **Life is a gift**: Each breathing moment is a gift from God. The biggest deception we humans believe is that we are in control of our lives or even our health. In reality, none of us know with certainty that we, or our loved ones, will be alive tomorrow or even an hour from now. Our lives can radically change in the blink of an eye. We are still alive on earth because of God's grace and not because of our own strength. Each moment, I strive to live according to God's will and remain in His love. With each breath I take, I am grateful to be alive, since I don't know when my last heartbeat will be.

- **Everything we have is God's gift to us**: Everything I have in my life such as my family, my education, the languages I speak, my profession as an attorney, my intelligence, my understanding, and my health are gifts from God. I was able to achieve many things in life because God gave me the graces I needed, not because of my own strength or merit. God gave me the support of a loving family, the capacity to learn and understand things, the opportunities in life to study and attend universities, employment, and the good health and perseverance to accomplish all these things. I took so much for granted when I was healthy. Now that I don't have my health, I need assistance to perform the smallest of tasks and movements. I recognize that everything I have had in life has been a gift from God, and I have no right to boast about anything or to take credit for it. The only thing that is mine is my will either to love God and accomplish His will in my life, or love the world which is governed by His enemy.

- **Suffering purifies us**: Suffering has been an instrument of purification from my attachments to material and worldly things. Due to my illness, I had to go through an intense process of dying to myself including my ego, my vanity, what others think of me, material attachments, many other worldly things and even detachment from my own health. People often say "*as long as I have good health, I have everything.*" Now that I suffer from bad health and I am still content, I realize that "*as long as I have Jesus, I have everything.*" It feels like I have been stripped down to my nothingness which has been a painful process but through it I found true inner freedom that I had never known before.

- **Suffering fosters union with Jesus**: In my daily physical suffering, I have been able to unite with our Lord Jesus in ways that I couldn't have done when I was fully healthy. I depend on Him for every movement I make throughout my day and at night. He is constantly on my mind, in my heart, and on my lips. With every single breath, Jesus' graces make the impossible become possible for me. Each day has become a living miracle for me. I have also experienced Jesus' profound love for me in the midst of my deepest physical pain and suffering. His love has elevated my soul to a supernatural level where my suffering has ceased to be painful, but has become joyful and light, strengthening my soul and increasing my faith and love. These experiences have shown me the strength of my spirit over my body. When I am united to Jesus, nothing is impossible. The inner peace that comes from a true union with Christ surpasses all human understanding and withstands all trials and illnesses.

- **Love is purified**: My love for God and for human beings has been purified. My love is not dependent on how I feel physically or emotionally. *Love is a decision and a state of mind.* I love others without expecting anything in return. True happiness doesn't come from the material world or from anything outside of us, but is the fruit of loving others by serving them and even by sacrificing ourselves for them.

- **Family's unconditional love**: Through my illness, my relationship with my parents has been strengthened and even healed. I depend on my mother and father for *all* my basic needs, such as getting dressed, bathing, cutting my food, eating, getting transferred to the wheelchair or bed, etc. Through this most challenging period of my life, I am spending quality time with them and experiencing their unconditional love and support. Ironically, I always thought that at my age, I would be taking care of my parents and not the other way around. They selflessly love me and attend to my needs, despite their own bodily aches. My illness has given my parents the opportunity to grow spiritually in graces and especially in the virtue of love, as they sacrifice their own time and comfort to attend to my basic needs. I love and appreciate my family more than human words can ever express.

- **Compassion for others:** I have developed compassion for the chronically ill and the incredible challenges they endure just to do simple things that healthy people take for granted. Unfortunately, most healthy people are not grateful for their health until they are struck with a sudden illness.

- **Appreciation for all the smallest things of life**: Before my illness, I did everything without much effort or thought and I took many things for granted. I used to take pride in accomplishments like working full-time while attending law school, speaking multiple languages, or traveling around the world. Now, my greatest achievements during the day are to transfer from my bed to my wheelchair without falling, or to lift my legs up from the floor to the bed without my parents' assistance. I value so many small details in life that I never even considered before.

- **The greatest paralysis:** The greatest paralysis is not the paralysis of the body but of the soul. Despite my physical condition, I feel an incredible sense of peace, joy, and love in my heart. I continue to serve others as much as I can, regardless of how I feel or the degree of my pain. Unfortunately, I often talk to people who are perfectly healthy and have many blessings in their lives but are paralyzed spiritually. Their hearts are filled with anger, resentment, lack of forgiveness, self-hatred, self-absorption, and other spiritual venoms. They are blinded to all the gifts that God has given them and often do not have the strength to get out of bed or enjoy life or their families.

- **Wasted suffering:** Nobody is exempt from suffering in life. We all suffer in different ways, but what's important is what we do with our suffering. We can waste it by complaining about it, becoming bitter, resentful, and angry; or, we can suffer with love and unite ourselves to Jesus' cross, allowing it to purify and sanctify us and obtain merits for others. Jesus told St. Faustina: "*My daughter, I want to instruct you on how you are to rescue souls through sacrifice and prayer. You will save more souls through prayer and suffering than will a missionary through his teachings and sermons alone. I want to see you as a sacrifice of living love, which only then carries weight before Me... And great will be your power for whomever you intercede. Outwardly, your sacrifice must look like this: silent, hidden, permeated with love, imbued with prayer.*" (Diary of St. Faustina, paragraph 1767)

- **Opportunities for others to grow in unconditional love:** As my disability has progressed during my illness, I have experienced the unconditional love of friends and even strangers who assisted me on so many levels. Some have provided me with transportation to the church, the radio station or even to airports, when I was still traveling. Others helped me in and out of cars or pushed me in my wheelchair, or picked me up when I had fallen to the ground. I have met many strangers who went out of their way to assist me. Through their generous acts, they have grown in unconditional love and earned spiritual merits.

- **Unconditional love is what matters the most**: There is no sense of ever going to bed upset with anyone or worrying about anything in life that is beyond my control. Nothing robs my inner peace. At the end of my life on earth, I will only take with me the love in my heart for God and for everyone I have encountered in my life. Everything else will be left behind.

I don't know what the future holds for me and I am at peace with that. What I am certain of is that Jesus loves me unconditionally and in my suffering I am more united to Him than ever. Everything in my life serves God's plan and gives glory to Him. Once I finally enter eternal life, I will see the merits of all my sacrifices and suffering. As St. Paul said: "*For I consider that the sufferings of this present time are not worth comparing with the glory that is to be revealed to us.*" (Romans 8:18)

Until then, I will continue to strive each day to love God and others around me just as Jesus commanded us on the night before His passion and death: "*This is My commandment, that you love one another as I have loved you. Greater love has no man than this, that a man lay down his life for his friends. You are my friends if you do what I command you.*" (John 15:12–14)

About the Author

Samia (pronounced "Samya") Mary Zumout was born in Jordan to a Catholic family. Her family immigrated to the United States in 1983, when she was thirteen years old. Samia attended the University of California at Davis and received Bachelor of Arts degrees in International Relations and French. She later received her Juris Doctorate from the University of San Francisco School of Law. Samia is fluent in four languages: English, Arabic, Spanish and French.

In 1990, after Samia studied in France for a year, she went backpacking throughout Europe with a couple of friends. During the trip, she traveled to Medjugorje, a town in Bosnia-Herzegovina (formerly known as Yugoslavia) where, allegedly, our Blessed Mother Mary has been appearing daily since 1981.

Her experience in Medjugorje was a turning point in Samia's life because she experienced in a very profound and life changing way, for the first time, our Lord Jesus' immense love for her. Our Blessed Mother Mary led her on her a path to living a sacramental life centered on the Eucharist. Samia has consecrated her life to serve our Lord Jesus Christ. This was also the beginning of Samia's own inner-healing journey and prayer ministry that led her to become a messenger and an instrument of God's healing love to His children.

Professionally, Samia worked as an attorney for over ten years. In her personal life, she has spent extensive time in the inner-healing and evangelization ministries since 2001. She aggressively pursued her own inner healing which later allowed her to minister to others on their own healing journeys. She was thoroughly trained in both basic and advanced courses in Francis McNutt's Christian School of

Healing Prayer and also Theophostic Prayer Ministry as well as other Catholic healing prayer ministries.

In June 2006, Samia felt a strong desire in her heart to write her first autobiographical book, *The Bridge between the East and West: A Journey to Truth through His Love.* While deep in prayer, the Lord Jesus confirmed to Samia that writing this book was an important part of her life's mission. It would draw many readers closer to the Lord when they themselves experience His healing love while reading about her life's journey. The Lord Jesus instructed Samia that it would only take her 30 days to write the book if she lived a sacramental life centered on the Eucharist, deep prayer and fasting throughout that period. Samia began writing the book on July 17, 2007 and the book was completed on August 15, 2007, exactly 30 days later.

Samia set aside her career as an attorney to follow God's Will in her life by serving Him on a full-time basis to bring His healing love and presence to His hurting children. She traveled for four years nationally and internationally giving her testimony and speaking on various topics related to the Catholic faith and inner-healing.

In 2011, Samia was diagnosed with diseases that have aggressively attacked her spinal cord: primary progressive multiple sclerosis (MS), cervical stenosis, and myelopathy. Over a short span of time, she became severely disabled—unable to walk, write, or take care of her most basic needs—and suffered constant debilitating pain and overall weakness. Despite her severe disability, Samia neither lost her joy for life nor her inner peace and her faith persevered and grew stronger. She has selflessly continued her mission helping and ministering to others through her weekly Spanish radio program "*Sanación del Alma*" (Healing of the Soul) on *Radio Santísimo Sacramento* and social media such as Facebook.

In the fall of 2014, Samia felt called to write her second book, *Total Surrender to the Will of God.* Through God's grace, she wrote it in two months by typing it with her right thumb on her iPhone.

Contact Information

If you have any questions or comments, please contact the author at:

Samia Zumout
P.O. Box: 189451
Sacramento, CA 95818

E-mail: samiazumout@yahoo.com

Website: www.samiazumout.com

Other Books by Author

The Bridge Between the East and West: A Journey to Truth through His Love.

In Spanish:

El Puente Entre el Este y Oeste: Una Jornada hacia el Amor a través de la Verdad

Entrega Total a la Voluntad de Dios

You can purchase Samia Zumout's books at:

www.booklocker.com

www.amazon.com

CPSIA information can be obtained
at www.ICGtesting.com
Printed in the USA
BVOW06s1636040417

480065BV00011B/70/P